DREAMS, BETRAYAL and HOPE

DREAMS, BETRAYAL and HOPE

MAMPHELA RAMPHELE

PENGUIN BOOKS

Published by Penguin Books
an imprint of Penguin Random House South Africa (Pty) Ltd
Reg. No. 1953/000441/07
The Estuaries No. 4, Oxbow Crescent, Century Avenue, Century City, 7441
PO Box 1144, Cape Town, 8000, South Africa
www.penguinrandomhouse.co.za

Penguin Random House South Africa

First published 2017
Reprinted in 2017

3 5 7 9 10 8 6 4 2

Publication © Penguin Random House 2017
Text © Mamphela Ramphele 2017

All rights reserved. No part of this publication may be reproduced,
stored in a retrieval system or transmitted, in any form or by any means,
electronic, mechanical, photocopying, recording or otherwise,
without the prior written permission of the copyright owners.

The lines on pages 115–116 from *Emperor Shaka the Great* by Mazisi Kunene
are reproduced with kind permission of Mrs Mathabo Kunene
at the Mazisi Kunene Foundation and Museum.

PUBLISHER: Marlene Fryer
MANAGING EDITOR: Robert Plummer
EDITOR: Mike Nicol
PROOFREADER: Bronwen Maynier
COVER DESIGN: Gretchen van der Byl
TEXT DESIGN: Ryan Africa
TYPESETTING: Monique van den Berg

Set in 11.5 pt on 16.5 pt Adobe Garamond

Printed by **novus print**, a Novus Holdings company

MIX
Paper from responsible sources
FSC® C022948

This book is printed on FSC® certified and controlled sources.
FSC (Forest Stewardship Council®) is an independent, international,
non-governmental organization. Its aim is to support environmentally sustainable,
socially and economically responsible global forest management.

ISBN 978 1 77609 092 1 (print)
ISBN 978 1 77609 093 8 (ePub)

Contents

Prologue 1

PART I: The Betrayal 19
1. Chasing a dream within the dream 21
2. History matters 47
3. What's in a name? 59
4. The biggest betrayal 69

PART II: The Hope 81
5. Time to dream ourselves into the
   new South Africa we imagined in 1994 83
6. Ubuntu as a healing framework 107
7. Rebuilding our society 129

8. Reimagined education and skills training 143
9. Reimagining and renewing our cities 163

Conclusion: Re-dreaming South Africa 181

Notes 189
Bibliography 195

I stand amid the roar
Of a surf-tormented shore,
And I hold within my hand
Grains of the golden sand –
How few! yet how they creep
Through my fingers to the deep,
While I weep – while I weep!
O God! can I not grasp
Them with a tighter clasp?
O God! can I not save
One from the pitiless wave?
Is *all* that we see or seem
But a dream within a dream?

        – 'A Dream Within a Dream',
         Edgar Allan Poe (1809–1849)

Prologue

Our beloved country has been unsettled. The dream that inspired us to a political settlement is being betrayed. The dream of a nation united in its diversity is fading. Those left in the dust of history as we proclaimed a rainbow nation have fallen even further behind. Our failure to complement our political settlement with emotional and socio-economic settlements has betrayed our dream of a prosperous democracy. Too many children and too many poor women and men are weeping for the dream betrayed.

People from all walks of life are bewildered. Some are increasingly and openly getting angry at the levels of abuse of power by political and business elites. The sense of betrayal by a government that was ushered in with such fanfare is pervasive. Even the most diehard supporters of the African National Congress (ANC) admit that the party of Nelson Mandela has gone astray.

The leadership of Jacob Zuma has played out all the nightmare scenarios of an unaccountable government. Significant parts of the ANC government have come to see the abuse of power and public resources as the mainstream political culture. Ordinary citizens cannot believe that the 'people's movement' has come to this. People are in despair in both the public and private sectors. Many ask: how did we get to this? Many young people are crying out for help in this time of despondency.

Are we ready to listen to their cries?

Are we ready to respond to the millions who are losing hope of rising above the cycle of poverty? Are we ready to hear the cries of the millions of young people whose dreams have been betrayed by a school system captured by corrupt teachers and education officials? Are we ready to acknowledge the cries of professionals in the corporate sector who are humiliated every day in their spacious offices by subtle and not so subtle racism and sexism?

There is hope.

A growing number of citizens of this amazing country are listening intently. Some corporate leaders are responding as the costs of talent wastage undermine productivity in their companies and growth prospects for the economy. They see their share prices stagnate; on their balance sheets and in their pockets they feel the abundance diminishing. Civil society organisations are growing restless and coalitions across sectors are forming to mobilise citizens to hold government accountable. Here are the signs of social responsibility. Like religious leaders who heed the clamorous cries of their desperately poor congregations, so it is our responsibility to act.

A significant proportion of young people are coming out of their post-1994 apathetic state to demand the promised access to quality education and training. They are insisting on an educational system that enables them to become proud, contributing citizens of the twenty-first century.

Even more important are the increasingly loud voices within the ANC from people who are outraged by what they see as a betrayal of their dreams. Veterans and stalwarts of that party have publicly denounced the affront to the dignity and memories of those who sacrificed their youth, their family, often their lives, for the democracy now being trampled on by the current leadership.

Why did it take so long for these voices to acknowledge that the dream of a truly free democratic society was being betrayed?

Citizens across the board need to ask how we sustain the flickering hope before it is snuffed out by anger and despair. How do we douse the fire of hatred and racist cynicism that has reared its head again before it consumes the core values of our hard-won freedom? How do we tackle the sexism and gender-based violence that is feeding off the persistence of white male dominance in our society and the impunity of privilege for those in high places?

These are the questions with which I wrestle in this book. I refuse to give up on this beloved country. I weep, yes, but will not give up. I draw strength from the growing number of fellow citizens who are equally determined not to let betrayal win over hope.

I spent the 2015/16 festive season in the Wilderness on the Garden Route where on numerous occasions I stood on the beach in awe of the roaring sea. I appreciated anew the wonder of the rhythms of nature. Watching the tide coming in and out at its appointed time cannot but ignite reverence for the power of the universe. The waves rise and fall in a rhythm only known to nature itself. I was drawn closer and closer to these unhurried powerful rhythms. I was reaffirmed in my belief that my country would rise to live the dream of a great society.

But the voices of despair, anger, discord and pain intruded into my reflections. Public comments and humiliating acts among citizens betrayed the toxic effects of unresolved racism and sexism. There were brutal murders of white farm owners, and brutal attacks on black farmworkers by white farmers. Gender-based violence had never been this widespread and this savage. Acts of racism and sexism were happening all over our country. Our efforts to eradicate these tendencies were null and void.

How had we returned to this country of discord?

Or had we simply been blind to its continuing presence? Where was the dream of a country united in its diversity? Why had diversity become a burden yet again, and not the strength we yearned for? Or had we been deluding ourselves all along? Was the rainbow nation the mirage that many had said it was?

I have spent much of the last three years talking to young people who are the majority in our society. Those between fifteen and thirty-four years old make up a significant 37 per cent of the population.[1] These young people across the gender, race and class divides seek assurances that the dream of a non-racial, non-sexist, just and prosperous democracy will have meaning in their lives, and soon.

Let me introduce two of these talented young people. Twenty-two-year-old Mapula is from Botlokwa village in Limpopo province. She is a top student at the University of the Witwatersrand earning every success with hard, focused work. Malixole is nineteen and from Queenstown in the Eastern Cape. He beat all the odds to be admitted to the engineering faculty at the Nelson Mandela Metropolitan University in Port Elizabeth.

Mapula and Malixole are both excellent students from village schools that had few resources. They overcame adversity to rise to the top of their age groups. Both are committed to becoming successful professionals and to contribute to their country's success as a just, prosperous democracy. These two young people are concerned about our society's ability to reach its potential.

They asked how a country as well resourced as ours could let them study in schools where teachers, who were absent from class, drunk on duty, and who molested pupils, were not held to account? Why did our society allow incompetent teachers to teach them? Why did our society allow young people to be in schools lacking the most basic facilities such as water, toilets and textbooks? Why did our society not give financial aid to poor and bright students at tertiary level, even when they scored high marks in matric?

Mapula and Malixole were acutely aware that they were among the lucky few. They asked me questions I had difficulty answering. For example, they wanted to know what a poor young person had to do to be assured of getting into and remaining in our higher education system. They found the stress of insecurity debilitating.

They were particularly concerned about how discriminatory and undermining institutional cultures were allowed to prevail at our higher education institutions more than two decades after the dawn of democracy. Is anyone paying attention to how uncomfortable poor black young men and women are in our tertiary system and what measures are being taken to correct what is not right?

I did not and do not have answers to their reasonable questions. Instead I asked them to challenge themselves, their peers, their teachers and their leaders to find ways of addressing these issues. I told them that I was proud that my generation successfully fought for freedom, but ashamed that we failed to make that freedom meaningful in the lives of ordinary people.

I acknowledged that the dream of a non-racial, non-sexist, socially just and successful society was yet to be realised. I implored them to make the dream come true themselves, rather than expect others to achieve this. But they were sceptical. How could they tackle such a tough task? How could they succeed where we had failed?

I also continued to have conversations with young entrepreneurs, professionals and public officials. The mood was gloomy among these talented and skilled people. Monde, a senior manager in the public service, talked about how he and his peers were trapped in unsatisfactory jobs, exposed to corruption and a lacklustre bureaucracy. He spoke of the anxiety among his generation of middle-class professionals who were forced to live above their means. They needed to pay for essential assets such as cars and houses without the support of a capital base.

In addition, black professionals felt that they faced scrutiny at all levels in their jobs and social lives. Those in big corporations felt they were constantly suspected of incompetence by their white counterparts. Those in politics believed they were scrutinised for signs of disloyalty to the governing party. They also had financial obligations to their extended family members, the so-called 'black tax'. Theirs, they told me, was a stressful life. A perplexing life. Was this what living in a free democratic country meant? Was this what their parents had sacrificed their lives for?

The failure of our education, health and social-security systems to reach those in need has placed an inordinate burden on the shoulders of those who have escaped the poverty trap. Yet they live in fear of sliding back into poverty and disgrace as they struggle to make ends meet.

The combination of pressures to maintain their new social status while sustaining a large extended family makes them risk averse. They will not challenge unethical and corrupt practices in both the public and private sectors as this could scupper their careers. This is a bridge too far. Theirs are uncomfortable lives. How do you uphold ethical values when to blow the whistle on corrupt behaviour is to risk so much?

I have also reflected on my own career over the last decade. I felt as if I had been 'standing amid the roar of a surf-tormented shore, holding in my hands grains of the golden sand and feeling them creep through my fingers to the deep while I weep', to adapt Edgar Allan Poe's poem. Yes, I wept for my beloved country and will continue to weep while we persist on the current path.

Many times over the past twenty-three years I have attempted to save at least one of the grains of golden sand from the pitiless waves by grasping it tighter. But I have also learnt to let go and to realign my efforts with the rhythms of nature. I have learnt to ride the momentum of the waves, instead of ineffectually fighting them.

There have been glimpses of greatness down the years. The engagement with Dinokeng Scenarios (a series of workshops by experts in a range of disciplines that looked at South Africa's present and future) between 2008 and 2010 suggested that we could live our dream if only we would commit ourselves to 'walk together' as active citizens, government and the private sector. African wisdom told us that *if you want to walk fast, walk alone, but if you want to walk far, walk together.* Walking behind leaders for the last two decades has not got us as far as we might have wished.

In the period 2009–2010 the majority of my fellow citizens broadly agreed with the diagnosis of the Dinokeng Scenarios. Without exception they said that they no longer knew how to 'walk together'. This was a startling admission given that our struggle for freedom succeeded due to the mobilisation of citizens across all sectors to defeat apartheid.

When I challenged this 'ignorance of how to walk together', many said that they had forgotten how. How was it possible to forget such an amazing human story? Walking together was played out in our streets, villages, churches, schools and on our factory floors. How had we forgotten? How could we have erased what was etched on the bodies and souls of so many here and abroad? Or was this deliberate forgetfulness? Were we wilfully forgetting?

Like Poe the poet, I stood there during those national workshops holding grains of golden sand. I then decided to tighten my fingers and mobilise my fellow citizens by establishing the Citizen Movement for Social Change in 2011/12. The Citizen Movement would help people rediscover their power to shape their own future.

It had become clear that the neglect of educating newly enfranchised citizens into the responsibilities of democracy was a costly mistake. A lack of understanding and confidence was negatively impacting on the quality of civic engagement. Both black and white citizens had no experience of how to assert their rights and discharge their responsibilities under a constitutional democracy.

Institutions and organisations that value high performance take great care to ensure that new entrants are properly inducted into their roles. So why had we invested so little in civic education? How did we imagine that the deep wounds and scars of both psychological and structural socio-economic inequities would heal on their own?

It could be argued that the new government had so much on its plate to transform the apartheid state that it could not be expected to cover all bases. But that excuse did not resonate with the reported attempts by some ANC leaders, including Professor Kader Asmal, then minister of education, to embed civic education in the school system.[2] He appointed a ten-member working group, chaired by Wilmot James, then a professor of sociology at the University of Cape Town. Professor Asmal's words in the preamble of the working group report in 2000 were prophetic:

> There cannot be a nation, there cannot be a democracy unless our education and processes of knowledge production and utilisation actively internalise values of equity, tolerance, multilingualism, openness, accountability and honour. There must be a bond that holds the parts together. There is a big task ahead to develop the values on which our democracy is being constructed and on which our future depends. Values cannot simply be asserted; it will require enormous effort to ensure that the values are internalised by all our people, by institutions, and by our laws and policies.[3]

We have failed to live up to the task Asmal set us. The descent into unaccountability, betrayal and conflict can be seen in the anger raging on our streets, in our institutions and communities. Such is the cost of not heeding his prophetic message. It was also puzzling why, after all the calls for a more engaged citizenry propagated by the National Development Plan (NDP), civic education continued to be ignored. There was not the slightest attempt to promote civic education. Was a better-informed and more engaged citizenry seen as a liability?

For a decade and a half I had been besieged by cries of anguish from many quarters to enter the party-political arena. After much soul searching I wondered if I could save even one grain of sand from the pitiless wave. Agang South Africa (AgangSA) was a response to these appeals. Many asked if everything was but a dream within a dream. AgangSA was a desperate attempt not to let go of the last grain of golden sand that I held in my hand. But desperation was not enough to secure success in the transformational processes.

Even the name of the party became a source of ridicule for white journalists: A Gang, they called it. This derision was all the more troubling in an African country where the only political party with an African name was the Inkatha Freedom Party (IFP). Not one political commentator or analyst saw fit to defend the use of an African name. Nor did black journalists put up a defence. It seemed to me we had lost a sense of identity and pride in our languages and culture. Indeed we mocked what should have occasioned pride.

The failure of AgangSA to become a force for change taught me valuable lessons. I learnt to see my fellow citizens without the idealistic blinkers I had carried from my days as a student activist. I also learnt much about myself. I understood more deeply why I had never been a member of a political party post 1994.

PROLOGUE

By crossing the line and joining a political party I betrayed my inner voice that cautioned me against it. I had successfully turned down Nelson Mandela's plea to join the ANC and play a role in his cabinet. I had argued that my independence was the best value I could bring to the transformation of our society. My time with AgangSA was a painful reminder that party politics was not my arena.

Many analysts have wondered why the majority voted for the ANC one day, then destroyed public property the next in an angry response to government failures. Over the years the ANC had effectively turned poor people into dependent, powerless citizens; they were its voting fodder. This type of politics had come at great cost to the country. It led to President Zuma feeling so confident about the invincibility of the ANC at the ballot box that he could say that the ANC would rule until Jesus Christ came again.

Protests against the failure of public services from education to health, housing and many other essential services had become events for the destruction of public property. Often communities were destroying the few assets they had. Violence remained – and remains – the only power that the powerless felt they could wield. The ballot box was not seen as a means of expression, of protest, of punishment. And yet, perhaps the 2016 local elections, where the ANC suffered beatings in significant cities, showed a glimmer of hope that may shine brighter as we head towards the 2019 national elections.

It was comforting to know from experience over the past two decades, affirmed by the amazing yet underappreciated work of scientist, linguist and African studies scholar Cheikh Anta Diop, that there was hope even in the darkest moments of human history.

He reminds us that: 'Humanity's moral conscience progresses, slowly but surely, after all the crimes committed in the past, and that is the opening toward others and a powerful element of hope foreseeing tomorrow the blooming of an era of genuine humanity, a new perception of humanity without ethnic coordinates.'[4]

This book is about how we rediscover such an element of hope. How we rekindle the dream we celebrated and willed into our consciousness in 1994. How to weave a society united in its diversity.

Part I of my book sets out the challenges as I see them. I draw lessons that might be helpful as we continue the transition to the country of our dreams.

I start with reflections of how I chased the dream. I concentrate on my passion for giving freedom meaning to those 'left behind'. This led me in a direction that can best be described as a desperate attempt to hold onto the dream. It documents how I strayed from my lifelong commitment to political activism as a citizen outside party structures. What were the lessons learnt? How are they shaping my ongoing engagement as an active citizen?

The AgangSA experience forced me to confront the process of human consciousness. Constitutions, laws and policies, important as they are, only provide frameworks within which the core character of a society evolves. Without attention to that core, little sustainable progress is possible in the attainment of a society's envisaged self. This core is all the more important in a society such as ours that has to be forged in the aftermath of excruciating pain and suffering by the majority of the population at the hands of a minority.

Forging a shared set of values as a society requires open, honest and tough conversations. Such conversations would help promote understanding and the healing of wounds – past and present. We need to embed ethics and morality in our social relationships: at home, at work and in the wider community. This is the unfinished business that needs to be addressed to enable an emotional process.

I have anchored the lessons learnt from history as a major focus of this book. It is a truism that you cannot get where you want to go without knowing where you came from. Again Diop reminds us that 'in the face of cultural aggression of all sorts, in the face of all disintegrating factors of the outside world, the most efficient cultural weapon with which a people can arm itself is this feeling of historical continuity'.[5] I will explore how as a people we have paid insufficient attention to history, including antiquity, to consolidate our cultural identity, our self-confidence and our sense of purpose.

This book also pointedly examines how and why we have inadequately used our historical consciousness to anchor our education system and thus failed to prepare young people to become competent citizens of the twenty-first century. The annual saga of diminishing returns for the high investments we make in our education system calls for a radical transformation of that system. The 'Band-Aid' proposals to rectify matters that successive education ministers have applied year in and year out have long been insufficient.

Ours is not a problem of lack of talent among our children and young people. Nor is it one of teachers who simply are not up to the job. Nor is it about parents who are not sufficiently engaged in the education of their children. Excellence in performance is about setting high human goals and values for our education system and working together as a society to achieve them.

Our dream of becoming a just, prosperous, democratic society must be founded on an education system that is geared to nurturing every child and young person. They have the right to develop their potential, which is why we need an education and training system that will cultivate the creative energy and talents of our youth.

To achieve this, what would need to change?

The student movement's focus on free quality education has triggered challenges to the status quo. For many of these students they are the first generation to receive tertiary education. They live at the coalface of poverty, unemployment and degradation in their families and communities. With the #FeesMustFall protests they have realised the enormous power they can wield to drive socio-economic transformation and shape their own futures.

The private sector would be making a serious mistake if it regarded these protests as government's problem. These student protests, like those of the 1970s, are the harbingers of sustained demands for fundamental change. No society can prosper these days without investing effectively and efficiently in developing the talents of all its citizens. It is remarkable – and alarming – that the private sector has yet to show its opposition to the mediocrity that has come to characterise our system of education over the last two decades.

Or, viewed in another way, perhaps the private sector has seen the systemic education failure as a business opportunity. Private school fees have rocketed beyond inflationary pressures because of a deluge of demand. Some entrepreneurs are investing in low-cost private education that targets the black population because they know that poor working-class and lower-middle-class families are desperate to invest every available cent in the education and training of their children.

PROLOGUE

Elsewhere in the private sector I suspect there are those who are secretly relieved that this underperforming education and training system provides an excuse not to transform their corporate profiles and cultures. 'There are not enough qualified black people to place in senior management positions' has remained a constant refrain. This could turn out to be an expensive form of short-sightedness with costly consequences for all of us.

Another important topic I address in the coming pages is the ability to sustain democracy in a country with structural socio-economic inequality. You need only look at an aerial view of all our cities to see that the resources are pooled at the centre with the vast townships and informal settlements on the periphery. It is here on the margins where poor people, sunk in squalor and misery, battle to survive.

Our cities continue to reflect the persistence of the apartheid socio-economic geography. Successive ANC governments, and the Democratic Alliance (DA) government in the Western Cape and in the City of Cape Town, have failed to transform these metropoles. The DA has governed Cape Town for more than ten years, yet has not shown the political will to break from the settlement patterns shaped by apartheid. The fraying of our democracy is exacerbated when we ignore our cities as sites of transformation. Each one of them needs to be liberated from apartheid spatial engineering.

The state of our nation's families also deserves much closer focus. The gap between the promises in our Bill of Rights and the reality of daily life for poor people is too great a gap for democracy to sustain. The rights of children, women and elderly people are constantly violated. Human rights and human dignity are not adequately reflected in our social relationships.

For instance, many workplaces do little to bolster the self-worth and sense of purpose of workers, including executives, to give them the space to exercise their family responsibilities. People who are humiliated and treated with disrespect are unlikely to become good spouses, partners or parents. The cost of dysfunctional families to our nation is incalculable. The productivity of our enterprises and our economy as a whole will remain suppressed until we have transformed our socio-economic situation.

Part II of this book explains my optimism about the future of our country. South Africa has always had the capacity to bounce back from the edge. Often, against the expectations of the rest of the world, we have resuscitated ourselves. Every time this has been because of individuals or groups of individuals rising to the challenges of the day and inspiring their fellow citizens to follow suit.

Think of Anton Lembede's, Oliver Tambo's and Nelson Mandela's generations of Youth League members shaking the moribund ANC out of its slumber and forcing its leaders to be more robust in challenging the racist system. Think of the women marching on the Union Buildings in defiance of the pass laws, the women who defined the rock that symbolises female power to this day. Think of Robert Sobukwe, founder of the Pan Africanist Congress, and his courageous anti-pass campaign that woke the international community from its complacency about apartheid abuses. Today the Sharpeville massacre of 21 March 1960 is etched in the memories of black people.

Think also of the young people in the 1970s who gathered under the banner of the Black Consciousness Movement (BCM). They spearheaded an uprising that led to the greatest sustained mobilisation of civil society ever seen in the country. Think also of the mineworkers who took on a powerful industrial-mineral complex and built the formidable National Union of Mineworkers (NUM) that reshaped the industry.

NUM challenged the mining magnates to move away from the century-old inhuman, unsafe working conditions and mining practices based on low skills and low wages. The momentum of the BCM spawned the United Democratic Front, which in turn created an opportunity for Nelson Mandela to become bolder in initiating negotiations with his jailors, culminating in the dawn of our democracy.

It is possible to reimagine and rebuild our society into the country of our dreams. It is possible to mobilise like-minded citizens to work together to develop a new human consciousness that acknowledges our history, culture and capacity to transcend our divisions. It is possible to build a country of which we can all be proud.

This book dares us to dream again.

PART I
The Betrayal

CHAPTER 1

Chasing a dream within the dream

Funny how a dream once dreamed embeds itself. It alters your view of the past, present and future, instilling a new perspective that shapes your very soul. Your values, mode of operation and allocation of resources, including the most important resource of time, all bear the imprint of the dream. Every fibre of your body vibrates to the songs, melodies and soulful tones of the dream. The dream becomes one with the self.

Ever since I discovered the joy of dreaming about a free democratic country to which I would not only belong but to which I would commit my life, I have become the home of that dream. It has been part of me for the past fifty years. It governs my every waking moment and every action. It is in my sleep, in my waking and in my understanding. My personal, professional and political lives are governed by the ideals of the dream.

The dream has shaped my every decision since my student

activist days in the late 1960s. My consciousness as a young black student came slowly. It seeped into my mind and soul like water percolating under the sand of a riverbank and only revealing its presence by dampening the edges. Having grown up in rural Limpopo with many unanswered questions, I was thrilled as they were gradually answered in deep discussions with peers. We were all groping for an understanding of how a majority could be oppressed by a minority for so long without mounting a process for systematic societal change.

We committed ourselves to being the generation that would find a way of understanding the barriers to freedom that kept us in bondage. We also committed ourselves to responding to our oppression and overcoming those barriers to freedom. We understood that many of the efforts opposing the racist system were at that stage led by white people.

Student organisations, political parties, church organisations, non-governmental organisations (NGOs) and the private sector were predominantly headed by white people. It did not make sense that those benefiting from the system of oppression could be committed enough to ending that same system. It made even less sense that oppressed people, a majority of the population, would passively wait for freedom to be delivered to them by others.

Psychological liberation

Freeing ourselves as black people from the inferiority complex imposed by a system that apportioned value and human dignity according to a colour code remains the most important stepping stone to true freedom. Psychological freedom from self-imposed limitations is an essential step to freedom from relationships that are based on physical and material oppression. A mind that is imprisoned by prejudices and negative characterisations instilled in it by others is unlikely to be open to freeing itself from oppression.

Stephen Bantu Biko, the founding president of the South African Student Organisation (SASO), put it most poignantly when he said, 'The most powerful weapon in the hand of the oppressor is the mind of the oppressed.'[1] What we did not know as young people at that time was that John Henrik Clarke, an African American historian, had reached the same conclusion about oppressed people worldwide when he said, 'To control a people you must first control what they think about themselves and how they regard their history and culture. And when your conqueror makes you ashamed of your culture and your history, he needs no prison walls and no chains to hold you.'[2]

My psychological freedom as a black person also awakened the woman in me. I was not only black and proud, but a proud black woman who became an agent of her own destiny. Growing up in a male-dominated society limits the bounds of possibilities that women permit themselves to explore. That freedom of a proud black woman enabled me to become a more active agent committed to shaping the history of my country.

I remain convinced that men are imprisoned by the dictates of masculinity: it entitles them to dominate others, especially women. Such an alpha-male masculinity undermines the self-confidence of both the dominated and the dominator. The dominant male in such a situation lives in fear of losing power and becoming dominated. He lives an insecure life. This insecurity leads dominant males to aggressive behaviour intended to scare off potential and real competitors. And life, when it is determined by a survival-of-the-fittest instinct, is fraught with conflict and negative energy.

The psychological freedom of oppressed people confronts the oppressor with the necessity of freeing his own soul from the need to dominate. And so as long as black people revere and emulate white people and use them as a standard of what is good, beautiful and progressive, white people will remain prisoners of their own prejudices. Superiority complexes in white people undermine their own abilities to honestly and rationally evaluate what they are good at as individuals and where their weaknesses are. Psychological freedom from a superiority complex is essential to consolidating our shared freedom.

White people need to appreciate how racial discrimination has given them an unfair advantage over their fellow black citizens. Accumulated material benefits derived from colonial dispossession, slavery and apartheid came at the expense of opportunities for black people in education, skills development and capital accumulation.

Contrary to persistent racist views, the differences in outcomes between rich and poor, educated and non-educated are not necessarily due to superior abilities or the work ethic of white people. They are the result of structurally engineered inequities of the racist, colonial and apartheid eras. Their persistence is also aided by the ANC government's failure over the last two decades to dismantle structural socio-economic inequities. Twenty-three years after democracy, the face of poverty and deprivation remains predominantly black.

The process of attaining psychological freedom is a painful one. Few are willing to undertake it. The unfinished business of freeing ourselves as a society from superiority and inferiority complexes continues to haunt us. Black and white people, men and women, variously sexually oriented individuals, as well as people of diverse languages and religious beliefs, avoid this healing process at high risk to themselves and society as a whole.

We cannot successfully chase the dream within the dream without attending to and completing this business of emotional and psychological liberation. We are destined to betray the dream we initiated in 1994 unless we are committed to the painful journey of healing ourselves.

Human consciousness is underpinned by psychological liberation. Psychological liberation unlocks the capacity to name yourself and recognise your personal power. The power that is then unleashed becomes the reservoir from which you draw the energy and resilience to undertake the arduous task of becoming an agent of – and for – transformation. A fully conscious human being is a citizen who not only asserts their rights and exercises their responsibilities, but is also seized with the historic mission to leave the world a better place.

Outrage at the betrayal of the dream

The betrayal of the dream that is embedded in me left me exhausted and hurt in the aftermath of the 2014 national elections. A walk along the Sea Point promenade is always healing regardless of your frame of mind. The vast expanse of the Atlantic Ocean generously sprays its salty perfume without discrimination on all passers-by. The kelp spikes the waves that lash the coastline with its own herbal fragrance. The rhythmic churning, roaring and splashing of the mighty deep calms my uneasy mind.

On this occasion I parked my car, put on my sunhat and set out in the direction of Green Point, with the setting sun behind me. Flocks of seagulls frolicked on the edge of the water picking morsels of seafood from the rocks before dancing away. Their squealing calls filled the air with an exuberance that brought a smile to my tense face.

It was good to walk in solitude among the multitude of walkers. We were all unburdening ourselves of the pressures that build up within the body, mind and soul. Of the faces that passed me some were deep in thought, others frowned, some smiled. Some were total strangers, many were familiar. We all shared this commonwealth and drank in the abundance it offered.

On this day I recognised a couple I knew well who lived in Green Point. We greeted and made small talk. But soon the man would have none of it. 'Why did you do this to yourself?' he asked. There was no need to spell out what he was referring to. His wife intervened in that very South African way: 'Noooo! You can't say that!' I rescued the embarrassing situation by offering to discuss the reasons for my doing the unmentionable at some other time.

Many friends and caring acquaintances had been asking me this same coded question. Many reminded me of my repeated vows never to enter party politics, so what changed, they asked. It was difficult explaining what changed because nothing had really changed. The same passion that drove my entry into activism as a student, a medical doctor, a mother, a researcher, a university executive and a global public servant at the World Bank drove me into the active citizenship that extended into the party-political arena.

What had changed was that I could no longer contain my outrage at the betrayal of the dream. I was outraged at the extent to which the post-apartheid government of the ANC had become addicted to power at the expense of the ideals of the freedom struggle. Neither the institutions that underpinned our democracy nor the national constitution were immune to the ANC's machinations.

Lessons from chasing the dream

I concluded my updated autobiography, *A Passion for Freedom*, with a recommitment to continue fighting for true freedom in my country. It was this commitment that saw me go through the bruising election campaign of 2013–14 to put the case for a political party that would focus on transforming our political culture. The male-dominated zero-sum notion of power needed, and still needs, to be transformed into a political culture that focuses on serving the public.

The choice of the name Agang (which means 'build' in Sesotho and Setswana) was deliberate. It was to refocus on the need to 'build' ourselves into the country of our dreams. The idea was to bring an indigenous name into the party-political arena. AgangSA also intended to focus on the citizen as the owner and agent of the constitutional democracy. That meant that the democracy could be whatever the citizens wanted.

The easiest entry point into party politics would have been to accept the invitation by the DA to join them and become the leader of their party. The DA had by far the best and most effective party-political machinery in the country. They had learnt over many years how to run the party to maximise their human, intellectual and financial resources to compete in elections. They also had a modern polling system that enabled them to monitor and test voter preferences and choices in real time. It was a well-oiled machine.

My discomfort with the gap between my ideals and their pragmatic approach to politics made me reluctant to join them. Attempts to close that gap through intense discussions over many months did not entirely succeed. It became clear that their commitment to transformation into a truly non-racial, non-sexist society with equality for all was a mental and pragmatic one. It was not a deep spiritual life-changing process. The extent of the challenge to right the wrongs of the past I felt required not only a mental commitment, but also a deep change in attitude and world view.

I yearned for a focus on structural socio-economic change that would make freedom meaningful in the lives of ordinary poor people. The DA prided itself on being committed to the 2012 National Development Plan and believed it was able to implement it more efficiently and effectively than the ANC. The NDP, with its limited view of what was needed, to me reflected the difficulty we faced as a nation if we were to live the dream of 1994.

The much-touted NDP was a great diagnostic tool that had high-quality data and analysis, but it fell short of being a road map to the country of our dreams. For obvious reasons, the National Planning Commission was constrained by the lack of robust, engaged, transformational political leadership to support the tough choices that needed to be made at the highest office in the land. Enabling major restructuring of our society and its economy required tough choices.

For example, the key driver of persistent poverty and inequality is poor-quality education and skills training for the majority. Unlocking high performance in education and skills training requires a fundamental shift in priorities – in this instance from protecting teachers to benefiting learners. Thus, if teachers (or for that matter public officials, even cabinet ministers) are to be held accountable, their performance needs to be measured. This process could have electoral consequences for the ANC as the public sector would no longer be acquiescent voters.

The government would also need to promote much bolder

partnerships with the private sector to create an environment conducive to on-the-job training. This could be done through strong tax incentives and direct engagement by senior business leaders. Civil society would also need to ensure parental and community support for the education and development of young people. None of these actions have been built into the performance and monitoring of the NDP.

The DA's traditional constituencies did not regard these inadequacies of the NDP as a major problem. They boasted, with good reason, that the Western Cape was better governed than any other province under the ANC. But their failure to tackle structural change in the province, and in the Cape Town metro, reflected their failure to prioritise and commit to undoing apartheid's geography. The lack of a political will to challenge the vested interests of some of its biggest donors undermined the DA's ability to promote fundamental structural transformation.

AgangSA was an experiment with a fresh start in party politics way ahead of its time. It was to be a demonstration of what transformative politics could look like, where the citizen was at the centre of the political engagement. Instead of members calling one another 'comrades', AgangSA members referred to one another as 'citizens'. We also adopted a code of conduct based on core values derived from the South African constitution: human dignity, equality, excellence, innovation and creativity. Young members of AgangSA, who were volunteers within the office in Braamfontein, Johannesburg, drove this 'Values Project'.

The idea was to build AgangSA into a party strong enough to engage in discussions about collaboration with others, rather than just focusing on my being entombed in the DA political machine without a constituency. The campaign approach was to mobilise citizens to recognise that they had the power to choose their leaders and to hold them accountable for the promises they made. We invested the first six months of 2013 in 'listening tours' to the poorest areas of the country to show recognition and to honour the voices of those feeling powerless.

There appeared to be overwhelming support for AgangSA as a new approach to politics. Young people were particularly excited about their voices being heard and the open invitation to them to shape AgangSA into a political party with which they could identify. The novelty factor was also a big pull to many people who were keen on engaging as citizens in determining their country's approach to politics. The focus on rural and poor areas attracted many poor people who had the opportunity to have their voices heard and their suggestions fed into the process of change.

I was energised by the positive responses we got across the spectrum. I felt that there was a chance to shift to transformative politics. Young and old, men and women, including those in the public sector, were enthusiastic about the chance for a new beginning.

For example, a visit to my own natal village, Uitkyk, in the Bochum area of Limpopo, drew a large crowd of residents who became excited about the message of hope that their voices mattered. They spoke of their fatigue with the many unfulfilled promises that had been made during election campaigns by local representatives of the governing party. They were still waiting for a tarred road (long promised) linking them to the hospital in Bochum, the local administrative complex. Their water supply and electricity remained unreliable.

We listened, and discussed how change needed to be brought

by the power of the vote. We sang and broke bread together. Many other villages and townships in other provinces were visited during the six months leading up to the launch of AgangSA in June 2013. The enthusiasm was intoxicating.

There were also wonderful moments in the run-up to the May 2014 national election campaign. The contribution of ordinary people in Soweto in Johannesburg, Mamelodi in Tshwane, Edenvale in Ekurhuleni, Khayelitsha in Cape Town and Phoenix in North Durban was heart-warming. Citizens across the country were eager to challenge the apparent impunity of those in public office. They were ready to overcome their fear of the retribution they might suffer from the dominant governing party for breaking ranks. They were ready for a new approach.

AgangSA was a successful experiment in a number of ways. Firstly, it awakened the nation to the possibility of truly democratic participatory politics. Many ordinary people wanted a new beginning. (Even today, many of these fellow citizens continue to urge me to make another bid.) Secondly, many were sufficiently moved to contribute a total of R50 million in cash and R30 million in kind to the AgangSA effort. A large number of these contributions were small amounts from ordinary folk. Many more would have contributed, but feared being seen contributing to a 'counter-revolutionary' effort.

Thirdly, and most importantly, was the mobilisation of young people. Young people at all levels of society volunteered their time and energy to the AgangSA campaign. Many of these young men and women learnt new skills that helped them prepare for their future careers. For example, Rorisang Tshabalala, a young entrepreneur, put his own business on hold to devote his time to the

AgangSA project. He brought his innovative mind to the campaign. Nyameka Mguzulo resigned her job in parliament to be part of the campaign, bringing with her valuable experience from the bowels of politics.

Finally, there were also supporters from the older generation. This surprised me. I had anticipated that they might be hidebound by their loyalties to the old ANC, but many joined in the early stages of the campaign. As did a successful global consultancy group which provided volunteer logistical services during the listening campaign, as well as strategic advice in the difficult end stages. We had businesspeople devoting their knowledge, skills and resources to strengthen our drive for support.

It was also a campaign that spoke to idealists such as George Lindeque, who had grown up in the National Party and had been part of the leadership of its most successful state-owned enterprise, Eskom. He sought me out at the height of the campaign and I found his strategic thinking invaluable. He became a partner I could trust when we campaigned in Soweto and other areas of Gauteng. One Saturday we tackled Maponya Mall in Soweto. I wore a track-suit and running shoes and he wore khakis and *veldskoene.*

George and I handed out pamphlets, spoke to voters and sat down for a fast-food meal. He looked at me with tearful eyes and said, *'My ouma sit regop in haar graf'* (My grandmother is turning in her grave). Here we were, a former anti-apartheid struggle activist and an ex-bureaucrat in the apartheid system collaborating to change the political culture in the post-apartheid era.

The outcome of the election was a great disappointment. To win two seats after all that effort was a blow to many of the people who had given so much of themselves to the campaign. So what went wrong? We will never know the full facts. But it is clear that many of the enthusiasts did not register to vote, and those who were registered did not vote. Our party machinery was not strong enough to ensure a high voter turnout among those who supported us.

It is also now clear that AgangSA was unable to convert the enthusiasm at public meetings into voter support. We did not have the capacity in most of the areas we visited to register, recommit and enthuse people to vote. With notable exceptions, the team was inexperienced at national, provincial and local levels. Youthful enthusiasm could not make up for the lack of organisational and campaign experience. And without that we were unable to initiate and build an organisation in the short space of fourteen months.

I also overestimated my power to attract, commit and mobilise people. I assumed that my powers of persuasion could out-argue the traditional deep-seated loyalty to the ANC as a party of liberation. The ANC brand was much stronger than I thought. The inextricable link the ANC leadership had created between the party and heroic leaders such as Mandela, Tambo and Walter Sisulu trumped any attack on the weaknesses of the current leadership. What people voted for were the heroic leaders of yesteryear, regardless of the poor performance of those in government today. The strong resistance from the ANC to any other party attempting to co-own the Mandela brand was not surprising. They feared this would weaken the link to the ANC.

Many of my friends and colleagues approved of what I stood for, but they were not ready to convert that into support for AgangSA. I did not understand the deep psychic attachment to a political party, or the difficulties of changing attitudes that have been shaped by decades of solidarity and family networks tied to party loyalties. I was clearly a novice blinded by idealism to the realities of the strong ties voters have to their traditional parties.

I also had to come to terms with the hard reality that fear remained a determinant of our politics. Many citizens complained about bad governance, corruption eating away at the soul of the nation from the highest office in the land to the local level, without necessarily being willing to challenge the system. The ANC had successfully captured the state to make those opposing them feel the 'cold outside', as its secretary general, Gwede Mantashe, reminded anyone who left or was asked to leave the ANC's fold. Citizens lived in fear of being excluded from the means of livelihoods and social networks.

I was cruelly reminded of Machiavelli's wisdom:

> There is nothing more difficult to take in hand, more perilous to conduct, or more uncertain in its success, than to take the lead in the introduction of a new order of things. For the reformer has enemies in all those who profit by the old order, and only lukewarm defenders in all those who would profit by the new order, this lukewarmness arising partly from fear of their adversaries ... and partly from the incredulity of mankind, who do not truly believe in anything new until they have had actual experience of it.[3]

I committed the fatal error of assuming that those who stood to benefit most from change would support the emergence of a new political party with a focus on the citizen as the centre of public life. That was a cardinal error in a climate where political loyalties to the status quo were paramount. For many the ANC was like a church. It was a religion. You did not change your church simply because you were unhappy with the priest. The 'people's movement' was seen as separate from its office bearers. Brand loyalty was the guiding ethic.

Moreover, the depth and widespread nature of transactional politics dwarfed any idealism and the politics of principle. What are you going to do for us? Where are the T-shirts? Where are the food parcels? Will you continue to give us social grants and RDP (Reconstruction and Development Programme) houses? These were the key questions on the campaign trail in many poor communities. Arguing that state resources were not ANC resources was akin to whistling in the wind. No one heard us. AgangSA could not compete effectively in entrenched transactional politics.

I also underestimated the effectiveness of the ANC's electioneering machinery. They had a formidable 'volunteer corps', including teachers and other public servants who simply absented themselves from their jobs and shifted into full-time party work for weeks before elections. These volunteers did door-to-door canvassing and distributed food parcels and other patronage from the public purse, such as Extended Public Works Programmes and social grants. The reality of poverty and the dependency on these handouts was not obvious to me until I saw it at work in the many poor communities we visited. It was hard to compete with a party that used your tax to oil its machinery. We were outclassed in the patronage department in areas where it matters.

The Independent Electoral Commission (IEC) also played its role in undermining our limited success. I was left with a distinct sense of having been robbed of votes. For example, in a voting station in Philippi in Cape Town, ballots were torn off bookbinders and handed over to voters standing in chaotic queues. This happened in full view of eNCA and other news media. The IEC refused to correct these irregularities. In the township of Langa, Cape Town, Nyameka Mguzulo's home base, AgangSA got one vote despite having many registered and active members and supporters in the area. How did this happen?

In the Tzaneen district, where AgangSA had significant support due to my eight-year association with the area as an activist medical doctor, banned and banished there during the apartheid era, the ballots were never counted. Gunmen burst into a voting station at closing time and tried to seize the five ballot boxes. Fortunately the policemen on duty foiled the attack and took the boxes to safety at the local magistrate's office. Surprisingly, the IEC took no action to retrieve the ballot boxes. When challenged, they argued that the uncounted ballots would not have had any material impact on the outcome of the election. Nor were there any follow-up investigations into this dangerous breach of the security of the electoral process. Why this dismissive view of such a serious criminal act that could have resulted in loss of life?

Similar irregularities were reported across the country, including black refuse bags stuffed with ballot papers. Whose votes were those discarded ballots? The IEC was unmoved. This was a surprising approach by a body whose mandate was to ensure free, fair and transparent elections. Each one of our complaints about irregularities was answered with an assertion that it would not have a material influence on the outcome of the elections. How did the IEC know that? What gave them the confidence to pronounce without investigating?

What, then, were the lessons from my disappointing foray into party politics?

Firstly, it became much clearer to me that it would take greater efforts to mobilise the majority of citizens to use the power of their votes to choose representatives they could trust. Despite slightly more than two decades of democracy, my fellow citizens, black and white, were yet to utilise the power of their democratic rights and responsibilities to shape the future they desired. AgangSA had less than two years to launch, mobilise and fight a national election. That was simply not enough runway for an effective and safe take-off.

The second lesson was that our politics were still too fragmented and colour coded. My attempts throughout 2013 and 2014 to convince other smaller parties to work together did not bear fruit. The United Democratic Movement was the one party with which we came closest to finalising a protracted negotiation process. In the end we did not clinch the deal and had to settle on agreeing to explore a post-election merger or alliance. This was most disappointing. Earlier discussions with the Congress of the People and the National Reform Party also led nowhere.

The failed merger between AgangSA and the Democratic Alliance was a public and expensive debacle. Our agreement on the process of merging AgangSA with the DA was undermined from both sides: reluctant AgangSA members and DA establishment figures. The proposed merger with the DA disappointed many black AgangSA supporters because most black people remain distrustful of the DA and regard it as a white party. Our members feared being dominated and forced to pursue policies they saw as unacceptable, conservative and protective of white interests.

I managed to convince the majority of members of AgangSA in the Western Cape and Gauteng provinces that the merger was essential to advancing the AgangSA agenda. As the majority in the population we need to use our power to initiate and manage the transformation process. My basic case for the merger was that the DA had the political machinery, while AgangSA had the ideals and policy options to drive a transformation agenda for the sort of society we envisaged.

Discussions ended before I could visit Mpumalanga, Limpopo and KwaZulu-Natal to canvass support from our members there. It also became clear that the DA establishment had an axe to grind with me for my earlier reluctance to accept their invitation to join the party. They were only interested in me as a leader of their party, not as someone wanting to initiate major policy shifts.

Many in the DA establishment were not ready for a merger that would have brought changes to the institutional culture and conduct of business within the DA. They were still too comfortable with the status quo of being an official opposition to risk becoming part of a majority black party. In short the DA was a comfort zone that they were not yet ready to abandon.

The surprise ultimatum issued by Helen Zille through the media on Sunday 9 February 2014 for me to sign up as a member of the DA instead of pursuing the agreed merger was a deliberate tactic to scuttle the deal. I was shocked because I had expected much more from Zille, with whom I had worked at the University of Cape Town (UCT). I was astounded that she could betray the spirit of our agreement announced only a few days before. I was still in the process of consulting with AgangSA members (as had been agreed and confirmed earlier that week) and she knew this.

AgangSA, like any self-respecting institution, had a constitutional requirement that any merger had to be put to the party membership before it could become effective. DA leaders, especially Zille, knew me well enough to know that I was unlikely to submit to ultimatums to save my skin. How could I betray so many people who had placed their trust in me?

There was another sinister reason for pushing me into a 'sign up or else' situation. The DA had unwisely decided to march on the ANC headquarters, Luthuli House, on Wednesday 12 February 2014. I would have had to lead the march on Luthuli House as my first act as a parliamentary leader candidate. Such a provocative act of challenging a powerful political opponent on their own turf could have led to bloodshed. It did not take much to realise that the confrontation between ANC leaders and DA leaders with me on the frontline would have been headlined as 'black on black' violence! It was a short-sighted political tactic with potentially huge reputational risks for all involved. In the end the march had to be aborted for fear of violence.

The DA establishment also played the fear-of-failure card. The easiest decision, even at this late stage, would have been for me to cave in and sign up as a DA member and become their presidential candidate. But doing so would have entailed betraying all those ordinary people who had placed their hopes on alternative party politics. Abandoning these fellow citizens would have added salt to the humiliation of poor black people, who are often forced into relationships of convenience in exchange for material benefits.

My principles and values could never have allowed me to abandon those who had pinned their hopes on AgangSA as a new beginning. They had placed their trust in me. I felt strongly that it was better to fail fighting a valiant fight than succumb to humiliation from those using their material dominance to undermine others. After all, you often learn much more from failure after trying hard than from a success that is dependent on you compromising your values.

The third lesson from the AgangSA experience was the realisation that the ANC would stop at nothing to remain in power. Undermining the foundations of our democracy, including the constitution, has become part of their operational plan. The IEC became discredited as a (previously shining) example of an agent for free, fair and transparent elections. One of the successful interventions that AgangSA joined was a collaboration with other opposition parties to force the IEC chair, Pansy Tlakula, to step down.

Like so many ANC leaders, Tlakula had defied the public protector, Thuli Madonsela. In this instance Madonsela found that Tlakula was to be held accountable for her role in the corrupt procurement of a lease costing R320 million for the IEC headquarters. 'Tlakula's actions risk a loss of public confidence in the IEC and also threaten the IEC's reputation as an impartial constitutional body,' said Madonsela. 'Tlakula's actions foster a perception from potential service providers that they can't expect fair, equal treatment from the IEC.'[4]

The problem in the lease came down to an 'undisclosed conflict of interest' between Tlakula and businessperson Thaba Mufamadi, who had an ownership stake in the property through his company. Theirs was possibly a romantic as well as a business relationship.

Curiously, the DA disassociated itself from the joint opposition parties' efforts to challenge impunity at the IEC. The official reason given by Helen Zille was that they could not see a credible alternative within the IEC with the capacity to run elections if Tlakula were to be forced out. That seemed a surprisingly defeatist view. How could we put up with someone who defied the public protector and thereby undermined the very constitution on which elections were based? How could we be so tolerant of someone breaking the rules, let alone her defiance of accountability to the public?

The IEC was further discredited by its failure to heed calls to ensure clean, updated and complete voters' rolls. Even after the Constitutional Court ruled in 2015 against it for its poor conduct of by-elections in Tlokwe in the North West province, the IEC still failed to clean up its act. Independent candidates in Tlokwe petitioned the Electoral Court in an urgent interdict. They had found that more than 4 000 names on the voters' roll had incomplete or no addresses and 500 or so names were unknown to those living in the affected wards in Tlokwe. A second ruling in February 2016 by the Electoral Court directed the IEC to complete a comprehensive review of its voters' rolls before conducting further by-elections.

The IEC has been seriously undermined by its capture by the ANC. The choice of predominantly ANC-aligned electoral officers, especially teachers who are members of the South African Democratic Teachers Union (SADTU), has led to its loss of credibility as an independent unbiased entity. The IEC has also turned a blind eye to the ANC's abuse of their incumbency and access to state resources. ANC dirty tricks that have tarnished our democratic politics include confusing uneducated voters by threatening them with the withholding of basic services if they do not belong to, and vote for, the ANC. The distribution of blankets, food parcels and other inducements has become part of the standard operating procedure of ANC campaigning. But in the face of this, the IEC remains mute. As I have pointed out, it is a cruel irony that the ANC uses taxpayers' money to fight against those campaigning for change to a stronger democracy. Yet this has become a prominent feature of our politics. There simply are no consequences for most of those caught committing fraud and corruption. Citizens have taken a back seat as the sovereign owners of these resources. In fact many have become the cynical beneficiaries of handouts bought with their own tax money. Ours has become a transactional politics in which public resources are abused with impunity.

The ANC also used its power of incumbency to undermine its opponents, even if that involved the malicious destruction of state assets. For example, the ANC political machinery effectively destroyed the Technology and Innovation Agency (TIA). As chair of the TIA, I had built very strong relationships with its senior managers as we laid its foundations from the merger of seven underperforming innovation technology companies within the Department of Science and Technology.

The TIA became an effective, efficient agency that worked with government at national and provincial levels, higher education institutions, other state-owned enterprises, the private sector and civil society. The TIA's mandate was to promote research and development projects into commercial products that would benefit our society. We worked hard to develop the TIA into a credible entity both nationally and internationally as the only purpose-built African technology and innovation agency. I resigned from the TIA after four years of hard work in April 2012 when my term ended.

As soon as AgangSA was launched in 2013, my former colleagues at the TIA were pressured into framing me for alleged corruption in my role as chair of the agency. Their refusal to testify falsely against me led to their suspensions and lengthy hearings before the Commission for Conciliation, Mediation and Arbitration (CCMA). These were aimed at draining what was left of their personal resources. Those cases have yet to be finalised. The TIA was left moribund. This was a further demonstration of the ANC's ability to stop at nothing to perpetuate its own power, even if useful initiatives are destroyed as a consequence.

The final betrayal related to AgangSA was the apparent hijacking of the party by someone whose values I believe were at variance with those that inspired the formation of AgangSA in the first place. Andries Tlouamma joined the party late in 2013 and from the beginning seemed to stir discord. He travelled the length and breadth of the country to our branches and left confusion in his wake. We managed to expel two other disruptive individuals who appeared to have joined AgangSA only to destroy it, but he survived. I raised the alarm about the links between his movements and disunity within the party, but my colleagues did not share my suspicions.

Tlouamma positioned himself into the centre of the executive of our Gauteng branch and disrupted it by accusing the hard-working members of wrongdoing, triggering disciplinary actions on flimsy grounds. During the final preparations for the elections he created tensions in the selection of officials for the party list. He lobbied unsuspecting people such as Sam Njela, the then secretary general, to vote for him at the Manifesto Launch Conference in Atteridgeville, Tshwane, to become a deputy president. This strategic position enabled him to claim the leadership of the party once I announced my decision to withdraw from party politics after the election.

My objection to his taking up one of the two seats in parliament that AgangSA had won led him to fabricate and lay a charge of corruption against me at the Brooklyn police station. He ran a relentless media campaign to besmirch my name as a corrupt, undemocratic leader who the party had to get rid of. The distortions stopped only when my lawyers suggested he retract his scurrilous claims or face the legal consequences. To add insult to injury, Tlouamma and a fellow traveller occupy those two AgangSA seats in parliament, earning member of parliament (MP) salaries, and I haven't seen either one of them lifting a finger to promote the philosophies that AgangSA stood for. I doubt he would know where to start. A question: who does he represent?

As I have intimated, my most important lesson of the AgangSA experiment was the realisation that I was not a party-political animal. I did not know how to play the political game. I had no capacity to compromise on matters I felt strongly about, especially matters of principle. I was and am an idealist and political activist. I remain determined to continue the fight for freedom. I will continue to mobilise my fellow citizens to assert their rights and exercise their responsibilities to hold those in power accountable. I will continue to chase the dream by whatever means are appropriate so that we can become a more mature democracy.

My reflections on the AgangSA experience led me to conclude that the heavy moral burden of being one of the few survivors of that original small band of student activists often pushed me into states of desperation. I became a lone warrior against the culture of impunity that has now engulfed our public life. A more effective way forward was needed to rescue the dream than a warrior with a band of supporters. What was needed was confrontation with the unfinished business of acknowledging the wounds of a poverty that had been engineered by racist and sexist means. The roots lay in our history, and still bedevilled the political economy of our post-apartheid society.

CHAPTER 2

History matters

The negation of the history and intellectual accomplishments of Black Africans was cultural, mental murder, which preceded and paved the way for their genocide here and there in the world.
— Cheikh Anta Diop[1]

Kader Asmal, as minister of education in 2007, emphasised the importance of telling one's story. He said that apartheid history was the story of the hunter and that it was time to hear the story of the lion:

> The lion, we have always hoped, will one day have its day...
> The lion will one day rise up and write the history of Africa.
> We know, very well, the kinds of histories that have been written by the hunter. Those books only serve the hunter's interests...
> We now want to hear the lion's story. We now want to hear the lion's roar.[2]

Ten years later the question is whether the lion's roar has been audible enough. What impact has the lion's story had on our ability to counter the negation of our history and intellectual accomplishments as black people? It would seem that whatever roar the lion has uttered has not had the necessary impact on the understanding of the stories of both the hunter and the lion. Or has it?

I have talked to hundreds of young people over the last three years about the state of our nation. Young people aged eighteen to thirty are deeply concerned about what they perceive as the country's drifting in the wrong direction. What was striking about our conversations was the limited knowledge these energetic, smart young people have of their country's history.

Few of even the most visible and audible student activists on our higher education campuses are able to draw lessons from the 1968 global student uprisings and the way these impacted here. The details of the 1976 student-led uprisings in our own country are but fragments in their knowledge. There is no systematic analysis of the context, the ideals and the critical philosophies that underpinned those uprisings. They may know the rhetoric and have scanty facts from the time, but that is all.

At the beginning of February 2016 I met two firebrands of the current student activist movement. This was a meeting at their request. They had three issues to discuss. First, they needed to learn from me what lessons they could draw from my generation's student activism. Second, they asked how they could frame their current activist programme to accelerate transformation within the higher education system. The final issue was how I could assist them in their endeavours.

I was encouraged to see young people rise to their responsibilities to be active citizens. The issues they were raising within the tertiary sector were pertinent and addressed the gap between our dream of a just and prosperous society and our daily reality. Why did we still have inaccessible higher education that was often also of low quality? Why was there so little progress in making the institutional cultures of our tertiary sector enabling of excellence and equity? Why had we been so tolerant of the inertia in the transformation of higher education over the last twenty-three years?

You had to admire the students for using the power of social media to mobilise against the stagnation of transformation. #FeesMustFall, #RhodesMustFall, #BlackLivesMatter, etc. But the challenge for the students was to define what must rise and stand in the aftermath of the 'falls' they were demanding within higher education. What was their vision of a transformed higher education? What was their vision of a transformed society?

What disappointed me most was that none of the student activists I spoke to had ever read and critically examined the history of student activism in their country. They had neither revisited my generation's activism, nor that of the post-1994 generation who challenged the higher education system to transform itself to align with the national political transformation that was under way then. How could you be effective as a change agent if you did not even attempt to learn the lessons of recent history? I tried to impress this on the two young people, without much success. They thought that it was enough to simply hear an account from me.

Even more shocking was the realisation that the more prominent of the two was a final-year political science student. This raised a question about the quality of political science teaching in our higher education institutions today. How could students graduate from our institutions without an understanding of the journey that led to our freedom? It was not surprising that they could not state what their movement stood for on one page. It was all very well to say 'this or that must fall', but it was much more difficult to articulate what was to rise and stand in their place.

What is the source of the ignorance of history?

Young people across the country complain about the inadequate treatment of South African history in the school curriculum. Content is largely superficial with little reference to new research on the subject. History is taught as part of social studies in the new curriculum and South African history is most often scheduled for the last quarter of the year. Interest among students in new material is at its lowest at the end of the school year with exams looming. The quality of teaching is often insufficiently inspirational to encourage them to read beyond their textbooks.

Many of our younger citizens know little about the foundations and evolution of our society, let alone that of other societies on the African continent. Few have been made aware of antiquity studies and pre-colonial history. Likewise, the analysis of the extent and depth of the impact of imperialism and colonialism on the socio-economic structure of our society is not something to which they have ever been exposed.

The history of the struggle for freedom has been reduced to the history of the victors who now sit in the Union Buildings. The coverage of the freedom struggle tends to be focused only on the ANC's role as liberator with little reference to the contributions of other anti-apartheid movements. The role of the youth in re-energising the struggle in the 1970s is underplayed, which means that today's youth are denied the inspiration they need to become architects of their own future.

Academic reviews of our history curriculum are critical of the quality of that subject. The first criticism is that the importance of history as a subject was diminished when it became diluted in the then new 'Curriculum 2005' as a sub-section of the social sciences. In one quick stroke, history ceased to matter as an area of serious intellectual engagement. The second problem is the poor content of the textbooks. There is little evidence of the rich research material available on the subject.

There is also no purposeful insertion of archaeology and palaeontology, and the role of Africa as the cradle of humanity in the history curriculum. How are we to inspire young people about the centrality of Africa in the human story and the rise and fall of civilisations globally? There is no analysis of post-colonial African history – successes and failures to aid students to place their country within the evolution of post-colonial Africa. Critical educationalists conclude that the ANC has replaced white Afrikaner nationalist history with ANC triumphalist history.[3]

Our education curriculums, including at the higher education level, with notable exceptions, also pay little attention to the history of South Africa prior to the colonial period. The struggles of indigenous people against imperialism and dispossession are still largely taught with a Eurocentric focus. The courage, fortitude and innovative strategies employed by locals to resist subjugation receive minimal treatment. For example, the role of people like Moshoeshoe in building the Basotho nation and protecting those scattered by intra- and inter-ethnic conflicts in the eighteenth and nineteenth centuries hardly gets a mention.[4] The reign of Mantatise, the warrior queen of Batlokwa in Limpopo, does not make it into our history teachings at all.

The role of missionaries as the servants of colonial conquerors is also not given enough critical attention. Missionaries continue to be largely portrayed as innocent bearers of civilisation among a backward people. Their active role in subjugating indigenous people is not analysed. The significant contribution of missionaries to the establishment of education, training and healthcare facilities tends to blind us to their role in entrenching cultural imperialism. This aspect continues to undermine the culture of black people.

Post-apartheid neglect of how our history should be taught and learnt is a major flaw that is undermining the foundations of our democracy. It is difficult to effectively heal the wounds of humiliation inflicted on the indigenous black population by the white minority without the affirmation of historical narratives.

Descendants of European settlers draw their strengths from their version of history. Alternative narratives should be available to young black people to enable them to reconnect with their roots and draw strength from the achievements of their ancestors. The neglect of history is not just a South African problem, however. It is manifest across the continent.

We all create our cultural identity by reflecting on and interpreting our community's culture and heritage. We now know that the collective identity of a people has three components: a historic factor, a linguistic factor and a psychological factor.

It is difficult to determine which factor is the most important, but it is clear that the historical factor is the cultural cement that binds disparate elements of a people's identity into a whole. Stories make us who we are. This is why the characterisation of Africa as a continent without history has had such a massively negative impact on its people.

Why did conservative Europeans negate African history so vehemently? What was at stake in this negation?

Anthropologist Eric Wolf tackled the assumptions underlying this attitude in his 1982 book *Europe and the People Without History*.[5] Wolf focuses on Europe's rise from AD 800 when it was an insignificant scattering of settlements to its dominance as a global player in the twentieth century. He argues that this rise was fuelled by geography and the capacity to trade across boundaries, and the political consolidation that built the formidable centralised nation states. These nation states went on to create vast empires across the planet.

Wolf also draws attention to the rise of the Muslim caliphate in the 1500s that was driven by their deployment of horses and caravans to subdue European and North African inhabitants of the time. His analysis challenges those who assert the inherent superiority of Europe's civilisation and technical expertise when he points out that European civilisation is a beneficiary of influences from other cultures, most notably cultures from Africa's antiquity.

What is to be done?

Cheikh Anta Diop, a Senegalese national, dedicated his life and academic career to challenging the negation of the contribution of black Africans to civilisation. He used his considerable intellect as a physicist, mathematician, linguist and anthropologist to document the rich ancient civilisation of the Egypto-Nubian region as the original human civilisation. He demonstrated how celebrated Greek icons – Aristotle, Plato, Socrates, Pythagoras – were students of Egyptian gurus from whom they learnt the foundations of their later work. He also made a controversial case that the failure to acknowledge the source of some of the seminal concepts was tantamount to plagiarism.

Diop was driven by a deep sense of responsibility to provide African people with history as a shield of cultural security against those seeking to undermine them. It is worth repeating here his view that 'in the face of cultural aggression of all sorts, in the face of all disintegrating factors of the outside world, the most efficient cultural weapon with which a people can arm itself is the feeling of historical continuity'.[6] He urged post-colonial Africa to transform its education systems to embrace antiquity's rich heritage as imperative in understanding Africa's contribution to world civilisation. Diop's thinking complements the work of many academics challenging the notion of European superiority.

The rise and fall of nations remain complex issues determined by multiple factors. The ascent and demise of the Egypto-Nubian empires gave way to others in both the East and West. The first Europeans to explore sub-Saharan Africa's west coast were amazed at what they encountered. In *The African Origin of Civilization*, Diop quotes German ethnologist and archaeologist Leo Frobenius:

> When they reached the Bay of Guinea and alighted at Vaida, the captains were astonished to find well-planned streets bordered for several leagues by two rows of trees; for days they traversed a countryside covered by magnificent fields, inhabited by men in colorful attire that they had woven themselves! More to the south, in the Kingdom of the Congo, a teeming crowd clad in silk and velvet, large States, well ordered down

to the smallest detail, powerful rulers, prosperous industries. Civilized to the marrow of their bones! Entirely similar was the condition of the lands on the east coast, Mozambique, for example.

The revelations of the navigators from the fifteenth to the eighteenth centuries provide positive proof that Black Africa, which extended south of the desert zone of the Sahara, was still in full bloom, in all the splendor of harmonious, well-organized civilizations. This flowering the European conquistadors destroyed as they advanced.[7]

The most significant damage wrought by imperial and colonial conquest was the cultural and 'mental murder' of indigenous Africans. The systematic looting of the natural, mineral and human resources of Africa was considered justifiable on the basis that indigenous people were inferior beings – in other words, less than human. What started as a convenient distortion of reality became embedded as a racist way of life. Reality and myth merged. The dehumanisation of the 'other' became part of the standard operating procedure for subjugation and exploitation. The legacy of this characterisation remains. Africa is often depicted as a continent that invented nothing, created nothing and contributed nothing to human civilisation.

Cecil John Rhodes, the most brazen imperialist of the nineteenth century, was explicit in his white supremacist views: 'I contend that we are the finest race in the world and that the more of the world we inhabit the better it is for the human race ... what an alteration there would be if they [Africans] were brought under Anglo-Saxon influence.'[8] The sad reality is that too many white people in the twenty-first century share Rhodes's nineteenth-century views.

The continuity that history gives to a people is their most powerful weapon against attacks on their identity and self-confidence. The most effective assault on the culture of Africans came from missionaries. Their insistence of separating African culture, customs and practices from Christianity had devastating results. To become a Christian you had to abandon your identity, symbolised most powerfully by replacing your African name with a Christian one.

In addition you had to abandon traditional clothing for 'civilised' European apparel. Traditional hemp textiles used to make garments such as *imibhaco*, colourful women's skirts, were dismissively referred to as 'kaffir sheeting'. Beads, the pride of African traditional attire, were also frowned upon. These items were the baubles of heathens and not appropriate for Christians to wear. Stripping indigenous people of pride in their culture and its expressions in language, dress and rituals effectively concluded the mental and cultural murder spoken of so eloquently by Cheikh Anta Diop.

The perpetuation of the lie that Western civilisation is the source of science, mathematics, astronomy, philosophy and biomedical practice alienates black students from these fields. We need to teach the history of science with reference to Africa's contribution which is historically well documented. Our children need to be exposed to black role models who are scientists and celebrated achievers, both contemporary and those from antiquity.

For example, how many young black South Africans know of Dr John Henrik Clarke (1915–1998), an African American writer, historian, professor and pioneer in the establishment of African studies at universities? As a professor in the study of African world history, in 1969, he became the founding chairman of the Department of Black and Puerto Rican Studies at Hunter College of the City University of New York. He was also the Carter G. Woodson Distinguished Visiting Professor of African History at Cornell University's Africana Studies and Research Center.

Clarke's views challenged the mostly white academic historians. Indeed he attributed their reluctance to acknowledge the historical contributions of black people to the systematic and racist suppression and distortion of African history. Clarke asserted: 'Nothing in Africa had any European influence before 332 B.C. If you have 10,000 years behind you before you even saw a European, then who gave you the idea that he moved from the ice-age, came all the way into Africa and built a great civilization and disappeared, when he had not built a shoe for himself or a house with a window?'[9]

Our teachers and their pupils often lack the confidence to approach mathematics and science as subjects they can master. Instead of tackling the root causes of failure by rigorously assessing the content of our textbooks and the teaching skills of our teachers, we opted to lower the bar. We introduced an easier alternative, called maths literacy, to boost pass rates. This was a triumph for racists. They could use this to continue their perception that black people could not think in three dimensions and were incapable of complex mathematical computations.

We need to reinvent the study of our history as post-apartheid citizens. Our history books are distortions of previous distortions. Imagine if we made the teaching of history a critical engagement between the teacher and learners to interrogate the traditional notions perpetuated in our historiography. Joy DeGruy, an African American psychologist and social worker, encouraged her fellow citizens to use the power of stories to rediscover themselves: 'Telling our stories can be redemptive. Telling our stories can free us. Story telling is an important part of our education; it strengthens us and builds resilience. It helps us put things in the proper perspective.'[10]

There can be no doubt that we have not managed to put our current reality in its proper perspective. We are not yet living by our own stories. The young people I speak to have no way of contextualising their daily painful realities in 'the proper perspective'. They struggle to understand why the face of poverty remains black when the government of the day is predominantly black.

Why are they continuing to live in the grinding poverty of townships and villages in a country with so many rich, modern, urban resources? Why is their education so much poorer than the education afforded to their peers – black and white – from the middle and upper classes? Why are many public officials, who are predominantly black, treating poor people, who are majority black, with such disrespect?

The story of the lion has yet to be told. The story of the lion after its triumph over the hunter does not seem to have the happy ending of transforming the living reality for its cubs. Imagine if we could turn to the rich African heritage of storytelling to establish firmer foundations for a future that would be more secure, shaped and built by a people in tune with their roots.

Forgiveness and not forgetfulness is what should have been the focus of our reconciliation process. Genuine forgiveness requires acknowledgement of what went wrong. The forgiver at least needs to know what is to be forgiven. This is why history matters.

CHAPTER 3

What's in a name?

Everything.

The introduction of Christian names during the colonial and apartheid periods effectively delegitimised the naming practices of indigenous people. African names are sacred markers that one generation bestows on another to keep them connected to their roots. Some ethnic groups such as the Northern Basotho (Bapedi), from whom I descend, have a framework that keeps the same name within the family across generations. One could literally reconstruct the family tree by tracing the names of children and grandchildren from a base couple.

The norms of naming children after grandparents, aunts and uncles knit the families together. Cousins share names with their grandparents on both sides of the family. The names are not only a powerful identity statement, but connect several generations. Each name has a praise song that situates children within the circle of their family, including ancestors. Names are a source of pride in African culture.

Christian names given by missionaries were often derived from biblical saints and other spiritual Christian ancestors: Matthew, Paul, Simon, etc. Even today, demand for names that are easy to pronounce by white employers, white-dominated schools and the corporate world spawns the most shocking and humiliating naming practices. Many poor parents give embarrassing names to their children: Beauty, Precious, Firstman, Christmas, Welcome, Felicity, Small, etc. For many it is a sign of higher social status to have a 'European name'.

Young African parents in our post-apartheid society often tell stories of how some white teachers in private schools put pressure on them to create nicknames for their children for the school's convenience. Many white teachers make little effort to pronounce African names. For example, Songezo they would suggest could just become 'So'; Myenzeni, 'Ze'; Mcebisi, simply 'M'; Molepo, 'Mo'.

The choice of some young people to rename themselves with 'cool names' saddens me most. At a meeting with university students in the Eastern Cape in 2013, a young woman introduced herself as Pretty. I asked her what her other name was and she sheepishly said it was Nandipha. When asked why she was not using Nandipha as her name, she said that she needed a name that was cool so her friends would be comfortable with her.

Further interrogation about how widespread this practice is yielded a shocking lack of pride in African names. Even within the circles of African students themselves, African names are losing their pride of place. I was told that to have friends you need to look and sound cool. African names are simply not cool enough for some young people.

Sadly even adults believe in 'cool names'. In 2013 I was invited to participate in a panel discussion in one of Cape Town's oldest synagogues. The audience was largely white and post middle age. The chair of the meeting struggled to pronounce my name despite my numerous attempts to coach him. It came out as Dr Ramafela. At the end of the evening an old man came up to me and walked me to the door. He said gently: 'You know, you could be so much more popular if you had an English name so people don't have to struggle to pronounce your name.' I was stunned.

The suggestion that I should use an English name was all the more shocking because it came from an elderly Jewish man. How could he have forgotten the painful history of the Jewish people who were branded with numbers in preparation for being incarcerated in concentration camps before and during the Second World War? Stripping a human being of their name and replacing it with a number takes away a person's claim to individuality and human dignity. My name is sacred and the most powerful tool to protect me against dehumanisation. How could this kindly man not understand that?

White South African journalists and businesspeople talk without shame about former president *Mobeki* instead of Mbeki, and of the celebrated African writer Professor Es'kia Mphahlele as Prof. *Maphalele*! Why are they able to pronounce difficult French or Eastern European names so effortlessly, yet remain tongue-tied by African names?

The neglect and undermining of African languages in our education system is also taking its toll on the position of African culture in our society. The disgraceful rules by some former 'whites only' schools, now euphemistically known as Model C schools, that prohibit the use of African languages on the school grounds continues more than two decades into our democracy. From pre-school to higher levels of education the message children are getting is that success is measured by how well you speak English. African languages have been relegated to the dustbin of elective subjects.

How can we expect young black people, the majority in our society, to grow up with a sense of pride and confidence in their ability to shape the future? If your name, use of your mother tongue and other cultural markers are regarded as the antithesis of success, how can you assume your role as a proud citizen? When the very core of your identity is under attack from childhood, how can you have a positive self-image?

Recently, a young black woman from one of our highly rated tertiary institutions confirmed my worst fears. She was raised by upper-middle-class parents, attended a Model C school, completed her undergraduate education at a good university and had just graduated with a master's degree. She said that she grew up with a negative view of everything black. Her neighbours were white, her schoolmates were white, and her most successful friends were white. For her as a black woman with black parents, blackness was associated with failure and shame. Her consciousness had only recently risen above her 'taken for granted' comfortable lifestyle. And now she is committed to challenging the status quo to reclaim her identity.

One of the positive contributions of the Black Consciousness Movement in the 1970s was the restoration of the dignity of black people by encouraging them to reclaim their African names. My grandmother's name, Mamphela, was reassigned as my first name. Aletta, the name given to my grandmother by Dutch missionaries, faded into the background. Our children and grandchildren are the beneficiaries of this conscious return to the source of our dignity and pride. But there is a real risk that the present generation of students is not yet conscientised enough to draw on this rich heritage.

Ignorance or lack of curiosity about African antiquity feeds the inferiority complex among black Africans and concomitantly the superiority complex among white people. As I have pointed out, racist notions of inferiority and superiority were nurtured during our racist past as a means of undermining the confidence, abilities and capacities of black people so they could not compete effectively with white people. And this has been going on since the arrival of the Dutch more than three centuries ago.

The psycho-social engineering that reached its zenith during the apartheid era has left deep wounds and scars. Likewise the structural inequalities deliberately created by colonial and post-colonial practices continue to bedevil our nation so that poverty, squalor and poor levels of education and skills training mostly have black faces. This predominance among this sector of the population is then seen as proof of black inferiority.

White superiority complexes are perpetuated by the predominance of white people among those with high levels of education, skills and socio-economic status. Many of their children and grandchildren have been brought up to believe that white people's superior intellects, work ethic and civilised values account for their success. The history of colonialism and apartheid as effective affirmative action programmes for white people at the expense of black people is not explained to these young people by their parents and grandparents. Consequently many of these younger white generations are neither interested nor encouraged to learn about the link between the legacy of racial discrimination and dispossession and the current structural inequalities in our society.

The disgraceful episode in 2014 of a drunken white UCT student, Djavan Arrigone, urinating on a black taxi driver captured this arrogance most cogently. He stood on the balcony of a pub, Tiger Tiger in Claremont, Cape Town, and urinated on the head of Puis Nomgcana, who was standing below. When confronted by Nomgcana, Arrigone responded that he didn't care, he could pee anywhere he liked, and that he didn't care if it was on a black man, because his father and family were rich.

Nomgcana, testifying in the magistrates' court about the attitude of this young white man, said: 'He did not see anything wrong with urinating on the top of a black man and he is not going to apologize for that. He kept swearing at me telling me that I am stupid. He told me that he was going to sue me because he has lawyers.'[1]

I am disappointed that my alma mater, UCT, has yet to take decisive action against this kind of behaviour. This is a university that was a trailblazer in institutional cultural transformation in the 1990s. Transformation included developing and adopting explicit anti-harassment policies. In 1991 UCT adopted policies to deal with occasions based on racism, sexism, homophobia and other deviant behaviour. It rigorously applied these policies without fear or favour throughout the 1990s.

A dean of the music school was dismissed during that time for sexually molesting young girls during their music lessons. Male students were expelled for sexually harassing or molesting their female counterparts. UCT became a safe space for all: women, people with a diversity of sexual orientations, and black people. Why and at what point did UCT return to a tolerance of harassment?

In the Arrigone matter, UCT management first said it regarded the incident as outside its jurisdiction as it happened off-campus. A later statement said that the legal process should run its course before action could be contemplated for misbehaviour. Predictably, having been found guilty of crimen injuria in the Wynberg courts, Djavan Arrigone has now appealed to the Western Cape High Court. By the time the case is over he will have graduated and left the university as a UCT alumnus and one of its brand ambassadors. This is a sad commentary on the failure of my alma mater to discharge its responsibility as a public institution responsible for educating twenty-first-century citizens about the legacy of apartheid.

History as a cultural weapon?

We also have the unfortunate situation that many young black people know too little about the history of their society to use this knowledge as a cultural weapon against racist attacks. They are vulnerable to manipulation by both racists and propagandists who project them and their ancestors as passive bystanders in the unfolding history.

Young black people also have little defence against demagogues who claim that South Africa was liberated solely by the ANC. Discounting the role of ordinary citizens in the liberation story undermines their capacity to claim their own agency to shape their futures. A sense of agency by citizens is essential to enabling them to hold those in government accountable to the nation.

Back in the mid-1970s, young people demonstrated a courage

and fearlessness in the struggle for freedom that caught everyone by surprise, including their parents. No political formation could legitimately claim authorship of the 1976 Soweto uprising. The uprising demonstrated the power of people who were acutely conscious of their human dignity and had pride in their culture. This pride in themselves gave them the confidence to become agents of history. We have them to thank for reigniting the flame of freedom. The ANC's negation of the key role played by ordinary people, especially the youth, was essential to its monopoly claims as a liberator that was entitled to rule.

Our higher education system has yet to give adequate thought to the promotion of the teaching and learning of African studies: language, history and literature. This is why students are legitimately calling for the decolonisation of the curriculums of our universities. South Africa has failed to fill the gap in African studies as a latecomer to the transformation of post-colonial education. The lion that Kader Asmal had hoped would write its own story has yet to roar loudly enough. What will it take to get African people to write their own stories and develop narratives by which they can live as a proud people?

Addressing this critical problem requires an acknowledgement of our missteps. The most fundamental error was our failure to transform our education system into something accessible and of high quality that could prepare young people to be effective, creative, confident, independent citizens. We came into the transformation of our education with a negative attitude. Our approach lacked the bold confidence to set high goals for our education institutions, teachers and students. We failed to infuse them with the values to match our ambition to be a society characterised by

Ubuntu – the 'I am because you are' philosophy – that is at the heart of the African philosophy of social justice.

Our anxiety to negate the racist stereotype that we are intellectually inferior led us to set low goals for our children and teachers. We were also preoccupied with emulating white people's lifestyles, so we undermined our own culture and values in our homes, communities and places of work. Success became measured by how well you competed with the white middle class rather than how you contributed your talents at home, in the community and at work.

The failure to ground education in mother tongue at the lower primary level makes the mastery of English and other languages much more difficult. Competence in your mother tongue is acknowledged worldwide as an enabler in learning other languages. It affirms your language and culture in the world of teaching and learning, thus boosting self-worth and self-confidence. Repositioning African languages in our education system is an urgent task.

Structural inequality and its pernicious impact on white superiority and black inferiority cannot be transformed by individual success alone. What is needed is a systematic dismantling of the structures that perpetuate inequalities. Education and training are an essential starting point. We need to focus on educating citizens to be conscious of their unique talents, self-worth and their role as contributors to build the type of society in which they aspire to live. The values of Ubuntu with its focus on ethics and morality should become more than a branding tool. Ubuntu should become a way of life to knit us together as a human race that thrives on connectedness.

Our political leaders need to understand the danger of continuing to undermine excellence in education by labelling black people as 'clever blacks' or 'coconuts'. This label undermines and discredits the pursuit of educational achievements among black people. It supports the lie that scientific knowledge is the preserve of white people. It also gives credence to the racist notion that educational excellence is alien to black people.

We now know from our studies of antiquity that the first astronomers, mathematicians and architects of complex structures were black people. So why demean educated black people? Is the ANC that desperate to maintain its political dominance that it wants to control what the majority of black people think? If not, why the insinuation that black people who are critical of some of government's failures are 'clever blacks'?

Tackling the legacy of superiority and inferiority complexes should become an urgent national priority to allow both black and white people to unleash their full potential. We have weakened the imperative of building a shared future as a society by burying our history. A history that is buried always returns to haunt the present.

CHAPTER 4

The biggest betrayal

The monumental failure to transform our educational system is one of the biggest betrayals of our democracy. How could we betray the memory and lived reality of the young people who sacrificed their youth, their careers and their lives in the 1970s and 1980s to confront the evil system of inferior education? How can we explain the failure of our education over the last twenty-three years despite the significant public resources pumped into it?

This betrayal is all the more tragic given that the ANC government has consistently allocated a large proportion of government expenditure to education. The total expenditure on education and training from 2010 to 2017 is R1.6 trillion. For the 2015 and 2016 fiscal years, the estimate is R240 billion. Yet there are children still attending school under trees. There are still more than 400 mud schools in the worst-performing province, the Eastern Cape. Some have received temporary container classrooms, but many do not appear to be on any government development list and are not even classified as mud schools, such as Tolweni Senior Secondary.

The *Mail & Guardian* and the Legal Resources Centre produced an on-the-ground report in March 2013 of Eastern Cape schools. The most disturbing part of their investigation had nothing to do with the overcrowded classrooms or the sight of pupils sitting on concrete blocks or the long-drop toilets; it was discovering that the pupils did not expect anything better. They had given up hoping for better facilities.

'What does it feel like to have to press your exercise books on your laps so you can write?' a reporter asked a group of pupils at Tolweni Senior Secondary School in rural Mount Frere. 'Because, you know, you don't have desks ... and what about the bad toilets? And there not being enough teachers?' The group was so quiet, the reporter was not sure they could understand English. 'A pupil squinted against the sun, shrugged and said: "But ... what else is there?" They walked away over the cracked ground towards their next class, dodging a puddle of water from a leaking water tank.'[1] Such is the betrayal of our children's hopes that they have given up dreaming of a bright future beyond their misery.

The extent of the betrayal of young people in South Africa can be measured by the death of their dreams of a better reality. The rhetorical question 'What else is there?' goes well beyond the absence of adequate school facilities. It tells of the absence of dreams for a better tomorrow where they would not have to bear the indignities that characterise their everyday existence. What greater betrayal of the promise of freedom can there be?

Countries spending as much as we do on education include Singapore, Rwanda, Iran, Costa Rica and Malaysia. These are countries with educational outcomes far superior to ours. Rwanda, in particular, has transitioned from the most brutal genocide to become a knowledge-based competitive African country. Those apologists of our poor performance who blame apartheid for our twenty-two years of failure need to explain why the terror of genocide has been transcended in Rwanda to produce excellent educational outcomes. Rwanda's young people are facing the future much more confidently than many of their neighbours.

According to a former senior public official who was in the Reconstruction and Development Programme in the 1990s, money was allocated to cover the reconstruction of all schools that were either mud or 'under the tree' facilities. According to the minister of basic education, Angie Motshekga, R1.5 billion was allocated from the RDP fund in the 1995/96 fiscal years for school infrastructure, including the eradication of mud schools. Yet mud and under-tree school facilities persist. What happened to that money? Who is being held accountable for this failure?

According to recent reports of the Department of Basic Education (DBE) there are more than 10 000 unqualified teachers in our public schools. The tolerance for unqualified teachers continues despite the awareness that education cannot rise above the quality of our teachers. Most of these teachers are in rural provinces and teach in some of the poorest communities. Why does the DBE keep on undermining the future of poor children by denying them the only proven ladder out of poverty?

To add salt to the wound of underperformance, many teachers simply do not show up to class. Of those that do, a significant proportion are unprepared and teach with neither textbooks nor notebooks. The DBE has over the years ignored court orders to compel compliance to provide basic education facilities and learning materials. Content knowledge among a significant proportion of teachers is pitiful. Teachers tested in a number of studies struggled to pass tests in the subjects they were teaching at various levels in their schools. How is it permissible to have such people in classrooms catering for poor children who are defenceless against the theft of their future career prospects?

The ANC government's low expectations of black pupils

The government's lack of trust in the capacity of black people to compete effectively in a meritocratic system lies at the heart of our education crisis. Years of being told that black people are intellectually inferior have undermined the self-confidence of those in leadership, who in turn project their inferiority complexes onto others who look like them.

How else can you explain the lowering of standards of education to the level where the DBE could pass pupils who achieved marks as low as 30 per cent? The ANC government in the early 2000s agreed that a pupil who achieved 30 per cent in three subjects and 40 per cent in another three could be awarded a matric pass or high school diploma. What the government wanted was high percentage pass rates in matric which could then be flaunted as a measure of success. The false sense of security this pathetically low standard created further shattered what remained of the dreams of young people. Fear of failure is what is driving this injurious lowering of standards.

The bitter fruits of the 'Freedom now, education tomorrow' campaign of the 1980s

The revolt against inferior education waged by high school students in 1976 was hijacked by underground elements into a broader 'making the country ungovernable' campaign. The generations of young people who dropped out of school, and their teachers who also spent more time off school and out of classes, developed habits of the mind that are difficult to unlearn. Discipline and professionalism are hard to re-establish once they are broken. Professionalism in teaching and the discipline of concentrated work went out the window. Striving for excellence became discredited as counter-revolutionary. Disrespect for authority became a way of life.

The cruel irony is that many of the children of the leaders of these 'ungovernability campaigns' attended private and/or previously whites-only – or Model C – schools. Poor children were sacrificed for the freedom we enjoy today, while their peers prepared for careers as members of the elite class. The continuing discrepancy in access to education contributes to the growing inequality in our society.

Traditional inequalities between black and white citizens are increasingly accompanied by growing inequalities within the black community. Access to opportunities for high-quality education and training are increasingly the defining marker of success. South Africa is no different to the rest of the world in this regard.

Our failure to acknowledge the impact of the tools and methods of the freedom struggle on many young people has left a significant proportion of them without the means for personal development. Some youngsters, driven to committing horrific attacks on their opponents, including necklace murders, were not afforded opportunities to seek healing. Necklace murders are particularly traumatic. The victim dies with a burning, petrol-filled tyre around their neck while the perpetrators dance at the spectacle. Many of those who were involved in these murders are struggling with the burden of unprocessed trauma. This unacknowledged distress haunts their souls and their capacity for respectful, trusting social relationships.

Similarly, young white men drafted into compulsory military service who were exposed to, and perpetrated, brutality against fellow citizens have also not been given the opportunity for healing. The trauma suffered by them in their training to dehumanise and kill their compatriots continues to haunt many of these men. Both black and white people live with the wounds and nightmares of necklace murders, torture of fellow citizens and other abuses. Why are we surprised at the high level of violence and crime in our society?

We should have heeded the lessons from post–Second World War demobilisation programmes and paid attention to post-traumatic stress disorder as it has manifested in many soldiers returning home from war. We should have had healing conversations about those traumas and the impacts they may have had on us so we could then empathise with our fellow citizens. We allowed ourselves to be lulled into complacency by assuming that the successful efforts of the Truth and Reconciliation Commission (TRC) attended to the deep wounds left by years of socio-economic human rights abuses. We were too quick to declare victory over the divisions of the past and the hurt they inflicted on the majority of citizens.

Our failure to tackle socio-economic structural transformation is now fully evident. Our society remains one in which white people continue to enjoy privileges and to dominate the upper classes, while black people remain the face of poverty and unemployment. This, among a range of ills, is largely because of poor education and training. We have to act differently.

Many activists who sacrificed their youth in the 1970s and 1980s have been left to their own devices to deal with psycho-social wounds deepened by a persistent lack of socio-economic opportunities. Many of the teachers in our school systems are also products of our post-conflict period. Their deep wounds from humiliation as professionals treated as inferior beings and remunerated at a lower level remain undeclared and unattended to.

We should not be surprised that so many teachers are struggling with alcoholism, drug abuse, HIV/AIDS and many other matters pertaining to ill health.[2] The disturbing numbers of cases of sexual harassment, impregnation of teenage schoolgirls and other signs of a dysfunctional school system call for urgent attention to the root causes of this crisis in our social mores.

The education system's core challenge is lack of vision and management

The ANC government has failed to align the transformation of our education system with the vision of an inclusive democratic society in which all citizens enjoy equality and socio-economic rights. Given the burden of our history we should have heeded Es'kia Mphahlele's advice:

> A genuine programme of non-racialism, in which we Africans must play a major role, tapping the best minds amongst other

population groups, must eventually lead to the Africanisation of our institutions of learning. This goes beyond simply filling our schools and colleges with majority blacks. It means revolutionizing the whole range of our curricula, giving them a new direction, a humanistic thrust distinct from the tyranny of didactic approaches that have choked up all the channels of education.[3]

The ANC's reluctance to 'tap into the best minds' to revolutionise the whole range of our curricula, giving them a 'new direction' and a 'humanistic thrust', has seen us miss the opportunities to Africanise our educational system. The alienation young people feel in our fragmented school system with the persistence of so-called Model C schools that are white dominated and have questionable racist practices is a logical outcome of this failure.

Highly professional and dedicated teachers are essential to the success of any school system. The teaching profession is about service to the public in a critical area of developing the human and intellectual capital of the most precious resource: our children. Unfortunately, the track record of the ANC government in creating and managing a high-performance public service is appalling.

The main reason behind the failure to manage the public service in accordance with our constitutional requirements is the conflict of interest the ANC faces. Teachers, police officers, nurses and other public sector unions are the ANC's alliance partners. It is difficult to see how ministers and other senior government officials can hold public servants accountable without being criticised by their political principals for jeopardising electoral support from these huge constituencies. In addition, some of these public servants are the political seniors of ministers to whom they are supposed to report. It is a recipe for an unaccountable school system.

The South African Democratic Teachers Union commands huge support among teachers nationally. Their members are estimated to be about 240 000 strong, in other words most of the national total of 300 000 teachers. If you assume a dependency ratio of 1:8 that rises to 1:10 with extended family members, you begin to understand the amazing power wielded by SADTU as a voter base. Add to this the gay abandon with which teachers spend time on union matters and ANC campaign programmes and you can then see how critical SADTU is to the ANC electoral performance.

In addition, the IEC has, over the last two decades, relied on teachers to act as presiding officers at voting stations. In a number of cases, some of these teachers have been found to be neither independent nor credible presiding officers. In the Tlokwe municipal election of 2013, teachers played a central role as electoral officers and campaigners for the ANC during school hours. The Electoral Court subsequently found that these elections had been neither free nor fair due to the voters being bussed in to ensure an ANC victory.

Given these three factors – low expectations, poor professionalism and conflicts of interest in the management process – how could anyone believe that transformation to a high-performance, accessible education system would be possible? Without a major shift in attitude by the ANC, from a focus on holding onto power at all costs to a focus on public service, there can be no significant performance improvements.

In January 2016, Minister Angie Motshekga described our education system as a national catastrophe, although not in so many words. In a speech delivered during a three-day education lekgotla in Centurion, Pretoria, she said, 'Simple: We allow mediocrity to spread like cancer to the highest echelons of the basic education system, thereby threatening the very foundation of the system.'[4]

What was striking about Motshekga's comments was not her acknowledgement of the shocking state of the education system, but that she was talking about an education system that she had presided over since 2008. One could be forgiven for thinking that she was just an innocent bystander. Why had she overseen this national catastrophe for so long without tackling the issues she identifies as the root causes? Why was she not held to account for this disaster? The simple answer was that the whole ANC government and its political machinery had failed our children. They had failed to tackle the structural transformation needed to create a climate for an accessible high-performance education system.

The extent of the catastrophe Motshekga referred to was inadequately addressed due to our preoccupation with matric pass rates, albeit that these were of poor quality. The hidden carnage lies in the undocumented dropout rates. Every year less than 60 per cent of the roughly 1.2 million who start the twelve-year school programme end up sitting for the final exams. What society can afford losing more than half a million young people's talents and skills every year for two decades?

This wastage of talent was buried in bizarre policies of not letting a pupil fail twice in a school grade. This resulted in pupils being 'progressed' to matric without necessarily demonstrating competence in key subjects. As I have already mentioned, another camouflage of failure was the introduction of mathematics literacy. Mathematics literacy is neither mathematics nor literacy. It plays into the racist prejudice that black people cannot do mathematics.

How can a majority black government buy into this perversity? The only way to understand this is to accept that many black leaders have yet to transcend the inferiority complexes that colonial conquest and apartheid foisted on them.

I recall Dr Stuart Saunders, my predecessor as vice chancellor of UCT, telling me how stunned he was to encounter the racist attitudes among corporate leaders in the 1980s. At the time he was trying to mobilise financial support for black students to study engineering at the university. He met with widespread scepticism about the prospects of black students being successful engineers. In those years, there was only one black African engineer in the country. He had studied nuclear engineering in the United States. Perversely, the lack of black engineers, resulting from the restrictions of apartheid laws, was taken as evidence of the inability of black people to tackle studies in the field.

One of the corporate leaders approached stated that he would not waste money in funding black engineering students because they were incapable of thinking in three dimensions. Dr Saunders was so incensed by this racism that he told me he stood up, pointed his long black umbrella at the businessman, and told him that he and his ilk were a disgrace.

The short-sightedness of people such as this corporate leader puts the country at risk of missing opportunities for change. Fortunately many other corporate leaders have supported UCT and more black engineers have graduated from its courses than from any other university. In 1994 there were 36 black graduates, in 2015 that number had risen to 170.[5] This increase shows what can be achieved in an institution determined to create equity and excellence in the transformation process.

PART II

The Hope

CHAPTER 5

Time to dream ourselves into the new South Africa we imagined in 1994

Without leaps of imagination, or dreaming, we lose the excitement of possibilities. Dreaming after all is a form of planning.
– Gloria Steinem, feminist leader

Our country needs to recapture the dream that ignited the hope and the pulsating energy of 1994. This dream enabled us to leap across huge chasms of angry divides to build a new society. The impossible became possible. Our courage to leap into a shared future made us set high goals to build a just society. Ours was to be known for its respect for human rights and human dignity. We embraced the African wisdom embedded in Ubuntu.

The glow of that dream has faded. Many citizens are questioning the very basis for that dream. Young people in particular question the adequacy of our ambitions at the time of our transition to democracy. Some even suggest that the iconic heroes of the negotiated political settlement betrayed the future in letting white people get away with murder – literally and figuratively.

Young people are puzzled that we agreed to a political settlement that enabled white people to continue enjoying their privileges without any acknowledgement of their participation in the unjust system that favoured them. Many young people regard our failure to secure firm commitments to fundamental socio-economic restructuring as part of the political settlement as a betrayal.

We have lost the excitement of possibilities that were so palpable in 1994. The rising level of mistrust across race, class and gender divides signals that all is not well in our beloved country. White racists have taken advantage of this mistrust and openly flaunt their racism. Many of them proclaim publicly that their higher socio-economic successes reflect their superior intellect and disciplined hard work.

Penny Sparrow, an estate agent in Durban, set the ball rolling in early 2016 by expressing her frustration with beaches full of 'monkeys'. On Facebook she posted: 'These monkeys that are allowed to be released on New Year's Eve and New Year's Day on to public beaches towns etc. obviously have no education what so ever so to allow them loose is inviting huge dirt and troubles and discomfort to others.' In defending her comment Sparrow said, 'I wasn't being nasty or rude or horrible, but it's just that they [black people] make a mess. It is just how they are.'[1] She was fined R150 000 by the Equality Court. She sees this as harsh and maintains she is not a racist.

In another incident also in early 2016, Pastor André Olivier of the Rivers Church in Sandton told his congregation that white people were wealthier than others because they worked harder and smarter. Tim Hart, then economist at Standard Bank, tweeted a few months later that twenty-five years after apartheid the number of apartheid victims was increasing along with a sense of entitlement and hatred towards minorities.

These comments were not just racist, but also revealed the impact of multiple generations of 'othering' the majority population. What started as a convenient tool to justify colonial conquest and plunder by a powerful minority – a tool that impoverished indigenous people – has become a deep-seated cancer. Like any cancer, denial is deadly for those affected. But cancer also disrupts those close to the affected person: family, community and work colleagues have to bear the burden of a sick person who lashes out at those trying to get on with the challenges and opportunities of life.

If only those holding racist views and using racist language would stop to ask themselves who built Johannesburg? How was the gold mined if not by black miners who toiled under difficult conditions to earn a pittance so they could pay the iniquitous poll tax imposed on them? How could anyone forget the forced migration imposed on black men in order to provide cheap labour for the likes of Cecil John Rhodes? How could anyone accuse poor black women of laziness when they left their homes at the crack of dawn to provide domestic services to white families at the expense of their own children's care? We need to acknowledge the gap in knowledge of those living in comfort about the real life experiences of poor citizens in our country.

The root cause of the refusal of those such as Olivier and Hart to acknowledge the privileges they enjoy is their denial of the compounded benefits of apartheid. They are blinded by an ignorance of the country's history and its impact on the majority of their fellow citizens. They do not see their privilege as grounded on a legacy of abuse of the rights of the majority by the minority.

Sometimes we need to look elsewhere to learn how to deal with our own ugly past. According to the celebrated Israeli psychologist Dan Bar-On, it was the historian Benny Morris who initiated a social healing process in Israel. Morris's detailed research produced compelling evidence that eventually led to an acknowledgement of the Israelis' role as perpetrators towards the Palestinian refugees of 1948. The task Morris undertook caused him serious trouble, and for a long time he could not get a tenured position at an Israeli university.[2] There is much we can learn from Israel, from both their successes and their failures.

It is time to dream again. It is time to lift our gaze towards a new horizon. Our 1994 dream was inspired by the 1955 Freedom Charter's principles adopted in Kliptown, Soweto. The aspirations of the excluded majority in 1955 were captured in their dream of a non-racial, inclusive society where all would share in the wealth and resources of the country. We now need to be even bolder in articulating our dream of what a twenty-first-century shared, inclusive democratic South Africa could look like.

We need to reimagine our society with the full participation of the growing energetic and talented youthful population. They need to do the work of reimagining in order to be a durable bridge between younger and older generations. The young people should co-own the new dream. This ownership by all citizens would enable them to commit to the lifelong business of building a society of which they can be proud.

We are now in the second decade of the twenty-first century facing new challenges and opportunities. These challenges require us to reimagine our endeavours and shape them into the great African society that Hlumelo Biko dreams about. In his book *The Great African Society*, Steve Biko's son concludes:

> Building a people-centric society characterised by its equality in opportunity granted to all citizens and thereby facilitating an era of shared prosperity through a globally competitive economy will be the greatest way South Africa can honour the men and women who died fighting for its liberation.[3]

Where do we start?

Each one of us needs to engage in the dreaming process. Our individual dreams will bring out a diversity of perspectives like brushstrokes on a canvas. Individually we will add the colour and texture that can only enrich the composite dream. But we do need the individual dream if each one of us is to participate in the process of reimagining and co-owning our future. Dreams are not the stuff of leaders but the possible futures that each citizen needs to own and cherish.

We need to reach out and touch, and be touched by, the dream of our reimagined society. It is then that it will shape and guide our world view. We will become the embodiment of the dream by not only dreaming it, but also by committing to its enactment. The dream will find expression in who we are, what we do, how we conduct ourselves at home, in our community with others, at work and in the wider public sphere.

We need to learn from people who are called to a higher purpose about how to live our dreams. Prophets, traditional healers, teachers and religious leaders become vehicles of their callings through the quality of their responses. Their lives become reflections and instruments of their calling. Their personal, spiritual and professional lives are directed at answering their call.

Pope Francis is a prime example. From the day he was ordained a Jesuit priest in March 1960 he decided to be an instrument of God's peace. He became a living example of what it meant to minister to poor people. When he was appointed as pope, he chose to live in a humble flat instead of enjoying the trappings of the luxurious Papal Palace. His choice of an ordinary apartment symbolises his dream of a church that identifies with poor people and fights for a more inclusive world.

Answering the call entails accepting a way of life that serves to actualise the central mission you as an individual are called to. We become the dream.

How then do we reshape our society to reflect the re-dreaming process?

Rebuilding our society requires the courage to confront the missteps in our attempts to actualise the 1994 dream. Two key foundation stones are missing from the building of the 1994 dream: an emotional settlement and fundamental socio-economic restructuring. Our celebrated political settlement is being undermined by these two missing elements. Cracks have appeared in the edifice of our society and over time these might put our collective future at risk.

What is an emotional settlement?

In the preamble of our constitution we committed ourselves to:
- heal the divisions of the past;
- lay the foundations for a democratic and open society;

- improve the quality of life of all citizens and the potential of each person; and
- build a united and democratic South Africa.

It is obvious that we are yet to heal the divisions of the past. The TRC attempted to address these issues by focusing on gross violations of human rights. Much more needs to be done to heal the wounds of our divided past. Professor Dan Bar-On reminds us: 'Reconciliation has a psycho-social component as well as a legal one, that of inter-personal justice.'[4] The TRC was inadequate due to its understandably limited mandate. The outcome of this has been further undermined by the government's inadequate execution of the second component of the conciliation process: inter-personal justice. Reparations that were promised to victims of human rights abuses are yet to be delivered to the majority of those wronged.

The President's Fund was established in 2003 in terms of the Promotion of National Unity and Reconciliation Act, more commonly known as the TRC Act. It had a total of over R1 billion: R800 million from National Treasury, R200 million from the Swiss government and R345 million from the Netherlands government. Private citizens in our country also donated some money to support reparations. Just over 16 000 people were paid out the R30 000 once-off agreed amount, but the process was halted in the 2007/08 period due to a lack of transparency in the disbursement process.

'That money was supposed to go towards our children's education and for health purposes,' Brian Mphahlele of the Khulumani Support Group said in 2013. Khulumani is a national organisation of victims and survivors of apartheid's gross human rights violations.

Mphahlele himself was tortured and beaten at Caledon Square police station during the 1970s. Furthermore, he said, 'As far as I understand, the TRC stated that if you sustained minor injuries during that time, you were to receive R17 000 per annum for six years and if you sustained major injuries, you qualified for R24 000.'[5]

We have a historic imperative to pursue a wider process of an emotional settlement as a tool to complement the political settlement of 1994 and to strengthen the foundations of our democracy. An emotional settlement is a process of acknowledging and confronting the traumatic impact of the system of colonial conquest, economic exploitation, including slavery, and apartheid as legislated racism. The consequences of this history affect both those wronged and the wrongdoers. Both black and white people carry the toxic aftermath of a system that undermined the fundamental human connectedness that defines us as humans. It is in our nature as human beings to seek connectedness to, and affirmation from, others.

The concept of emotional settlement embodies contradictory spheres of engagement: *emotional issues* of the heart and sensibilities; and *transactional issues* of striking a deal to settle a dispute. Or, to use Dan Bar-On's characterisation, an emotional settlement has both a *psycho-social* component and a legal one of *inter-personal justice*. How can we approach this in a manner that does justice to both elements of the concept – the emotional and the transactional?

Can a society engage in a process that involves emotions and leads to the open sharing of how individuals, families, communities and wider sub-groups feel about matters as sensitive and contested as the legacy of our past? Are we ready to examine our conduct as a people in the here and now? People from all walks of life tend to be reticent about opening up the inner world of emotions to others even within the intimacy of home and family. What would motivate the majority of citizens to willingly participate in such a process?

Is it possible that we could conduct reasoned conversations about matters that are likely to inflame emotions? How could those who feel that the past is past and should be let go be convinced of the need to revisit that past? How would those still dealing with that past restrain themselves in the face of the reticence of those wrongdoers not ready for such a reckoning?

We might be assisted in the exploration of an emotional settlement by learning from other post-conflict societies that recognised the value of dealing with the past in order to loosen its grip on the present and the future. None of these societies came into such processes willing to engage in a manner that challenged dearly held views about the past. Even fewer were willing to break taboos about matters previous generations held dear. Breaking with long-held wisdom about who you are and who the 'other' is, is a painful and difficult process.

I am indebted to George Lindeque for coining the phrase 'emotional settlement'. Lindeque participated in the To Reflect and Trust (TRT) workshops conducted in 1997/98 by Dan Bar-On, a specialist on the psychological and moral after-effects of the Holocaust on the children of both victims and perpetrators. In 1987, Bar-On travelled to Germany, interviewed children of Nazi criminals and wrote *Legacy of Silence: Encounters with Children of the Third Reich*.[6]

After much reflection, some of Bar-On's German research participants decided to form a self-help group that convened on a regular basis. In 1992 he suggested that they interact with a group of Holocaust survivors. This became the group To Reflect and Trust, where children of Holocaust survivors and children of Nazi perpetrators met. Later, they expanded to groups in other conflict areas (South Africa, Northern Ireland and Israel/Palestine). George Lindeque was one of the few South Africans invited to participate in the TRT workshops.

Bar-On's experience of healing stories is that we need to listen to all stories. 'A good story is one that both groups could contain emotionally and cognitively, despite the continuing struggle between them,' he wrote. 'This was a basis of a common understanding and feeling, the beginning of collective memory for people who clung to exclusive memories.'[7]

Our individual and collective stories have the power to enable a better understanding of who we are as a people. We need to explore and acknowledge the extent of our diversity and how we build a unity in this diverse society that goes beyond rhetoric. We need to acknowledge that twenty-three years of rhetoric has not brought us as far as we might have wished. We need to build trust across the boundaries of the identities we have assumed over the centuries. We need to reflect on what we have missed or what we have distorted in our environments to sustain the 'othering' of our fellow citizens.

Critically important also is the construction of a new identity as South Africans. That has yet to occur in an unselfconscious way. We have still to own the identity of citizenship – we remain victims and victimisers. Hearing all the voices would help us acknowledge our silences and our inability to listen carefully to our fellow citizens. As a male-dominated society we need to develop the habit of listening to women's voices and the voices of young people. We can learn a lot more from them than we have done in the last twenty-three years.

We need to raise our consciousness as citizens of a constitutional democracy and learn to embrace its values. Laying the foundations of a shared future requires work that will take us deep into ourselves so we can confront the reality of the stories we live by – both those told and untold. It is when we acknowledge our weaknesses alongside our strengths that we will develop empathy for weakness in others. Being kind to our own weaknesses will help us be more empathetic to others.

George Lindeque and I work together to explore this concept of 'emotional settlement' in the South African context. We believe that this could be a way of reigniting a reimagination of our country into a place of which we can be proud. We believe that a process of emotional settlement could regenerate the energy that saw us defy the odds to reach across our angry divides to achieve a political settlement in the early 1990s. It is our view that our political settlement is in serious danger of being undermined by the continuing anger, shame, guilt, denial and fear that simmers just below the surface of our society.

Lindeque's own story is that of a man who grew up in a typical Afrikaner family, steeped in its culture. His mother, referred to as Granny by the family, was a principled English-speaking woman who taught her children ethics and morality in that time of an unethical apartheid regime. He acknowledges the benefits he enjoyed from being a white male. Although he was a member of the Afrikaner Broederbond, he insists that he did not take advantage of the privileges of this network. He rose in the ranks of the apartheid bureaucracy to become secretary to Hilgard Muller, then foreign minister. He witnessed at close quarters Prime Minister Verwoerd's assassination in parliament.

Lindeque ended his successful career as the executive director for human resources at Eskom. He played a major role in leading Eskom's transformation in preparation for the transition to democracy. He is passionate about the need to have the work of an emotional settlement done so we can heal the wounds inflicted on the majority by the minority.

What are the lessons from nations that have not reckoned with the past?

The United States is an interesting example of a country that, despite positioning itself as 'the land of the free and the home of the brave', continues to struggle with the legacy of slavery. The celebrated American dream is not yet evident in the lives of many descendants of former slaves. Despite the gains of the Civil Rights Movement under the inspirational leadership of Martin Luther King, the African American community remains over-represented among those living in poverty and despair, those in prison, and among the unemployed. Washington DC, the nation's capital, has people living in abject poverty on Capitol Hill's doorstep, in the majority black neighbourhood of Southeast.

In *Post Traumatic Slavery Syndrome*, Joy DeGruy shares experiences of the US that could be immensely helpful to us as we seek our own healing. She ends her book with a long quote from notes written in 1781 by the American founding father and slave owner

Thomas Jefferson. Jefferson reflected on his fears about the impact of slavery on descendants of both slaves and slave owners:

> The man must be a prodigy who can retain his manners and morals undepraved by such circumstances. And with what execration should the statesman be loaded, who permitting one half the citizens thus to trample on the rights of the other, transforms those into despots, and these into enemies, destroys the morals of the one part, and the amor patriae [love of country] of the other... And can the liberties of a nation be thought secure when we have removed their only firm basis, a conviction in the minds of the people that these liberties are of the gift of God?[8]

It is extraordinary that despite his own reflections, Jefferson would continue to hold slaves for so many years afterwards. Slaves were only legally emancipated in the US in 1863, a full twenty-five years after the Cape Colony's emancipation of its own slaves. Americans continue to pay a high cost for their failure to heed Jefferson's concerns about the need to confront the implications of the impact of slavery on the morals and security of their nation. More than two centuries later African Americans still need to remind the descendants of slave owners that 'black lives matter'! That anyone should need to be reminded that human life matters is a grave commentary on the damage to their morality by the legacy of slavery.

Thomas Jefferson's fears that slavery would undermine the behaviour of slave owners, putting them at risk of acting in ways that displayed depravity, seem to have been prophetic. Little did he realise that the assault on the morality of those involved in enslaving others would persist across multiple generations. A significant number of white American police officers respond to any black male, whatever their age, as a threat. A black boy playing with a toy gun is immediately shot as if he is a terror suspect. How can these wounds be healed?

DeGruy uses Jefferson's reflections to examine how the unattended post-traumatic slave syndrome has affected African Americans. Her observations resonate with our own experiences over the past twenty-three years. As an African American DeGruy is witness to the impact of the syndrome on her own family, her community and the wider American society. She describes how the humiliation of slavery and the racist Jim Crow laws that followed has left deep wounds.

Neuroscience is providing even more validation of the importance of paying attention to 'social pain' and its impact on the well-being of those affected. Naomi Eisenberger, a professor in the social psychology programme at the University of California, Los Angeles, describes social pain this way:

> When I think of the work on social pain, and showing that some of the same neural regions that are involved in physical pain are involved in social pain, that can be very validating for people. For anyone who's felt the pain of losing somebody or who's felt the hurt feelings that come from being ostracized or bullied, there's something very validating in seeing this scientific work that shows it's not just in our head. It is in our head because it's in our brain. It's not just in our head, there is something biological going on that's interpreting the pain of social rejection as something that really is a painful experience.[9]

It is no longer in dispute that when some people speak of 'black pain' they are reflecting the hurt they feel from being marginalised in a society that was meant to be an open, non-racial democracy. They feel the pain of betrayal by those entrusted with making freedom a reality in their lives. They also feel the pain of the continuing humiliation under what they see as the mocking gaze of white people who continue to enjoy the privileges of their position in society. A position it is worth remembering that comes about because of successive 'affirmative action programmes' by white minority governments to advance their social standing. Humiliation undermines the fundamental core of what it means to be human. Self-esteem is at the core of our being. Self-esteem is the most important enabler of a sense of well-being, and of the capacity for social relationships.

DeGruy asserts that the impact of social pain on self-esteem in the US has led to the phenomenon of 'vacant self-esteem'. She believes that African American men seem to bear the brunt of vacant self-esteem:

> Perhaps when we do not have enough self-esteem the idea of manhood is all we have left. Perhaps when for centuries we have not been allowed to be 'men' our concept of manhood has yet to mature. Perhaps our sense of who we are and what we are leads us to perceive any minor slight as an assault on our very core. And when our core is in danger we respond in anger, rage and sometimes violence. And this behaviour often results in behaviours that undermine much of what we are working to accomplish.[10]

It is not surprising that men would bear the brunt of vacant self-esteem in a society that is so deeply male dominated. Slave masters made it a habit to humiliate male slaves in front of their families. Demeaning chores, public flogging, and rape of their daughters and sometimes wives were used to demonstrate that they were not real men. These humiliating acts were all intended to emasculate black men.[11]

During the apartheid era our fathers and other male relatives were often humiliated. Their inability to be protectors of their families not only distressed many black men, but also made them feel totally unmanly. White policemen would simply kick the door in and walk into black homes at will. In addition, our fathers and grandfathers were called 'boys' in front of their own families. Being called a 'boy' as an adult man is the ultimate insult in traditional African society. Traditional men go to great lengths to be initiated into manhood to ensure that they become respectable as real men. To add insult to injury, white people young enough to be their own children would also call our fathers and grandfathers 'boys'. The cumulative damage of this humiliation is incalculable.

In our own society, descendants of colonial conquerors, slave owners and enforcers of apartheid's discriminatory laws that deliberately impoverished as they humiliated continue to struggle to relate to black people as equals. What impact has this multi-generational system that dehumanised the majority population had on the manners and morals of those who were involved and their descendants? The benefits of that system are also multi-generational. How do we acknowledge and deal with this reality?

A growing number of white people feel increasingly bewildered by what they regard as unfair demands for them to acknowledge that their privileged lives have come at the expense of the historical and ongoing deprivation of the majority of their fellow citizens. Many of these white compatriots argue that they were too young to have been part of the apartheid state. They plead that our society should accept the status quo, and just move on.

These white compatriots may benefit from the example of a young German man who undertook the task of making amends with descendants of Holocaust victims. He understood that memories are laid down in our minds and shape our identity. Memories radiate the energy that flows into our social relationships. We can and must acknowledge our memories – conscious and unconscious. Conscious memories are established through lived experiences. Unconscious memories are imprinted on our psyche by association with those who carry direct experiences of traumatic events. Memories, however accumulated, shape who we are.

A BBC magazine programme tells the story of how Rainer Höss went in search of forgiveness from the Israeli children whose relatives his Nazi grandfather had exterminated. His grandfather was Rudolf Franz Ferdinand Höss, the longest-serving commander of Auschwitz concentration camp. He introduced pesticide to the killing process which accelerated the number of deaths to 2 000 people every hour.

Rainer could not erase the memory of a garden 'gate to hell' through which his grandfather walked to and from work every day. He was too young to know that his grandfather's 'work' was exterminating fellow human beings simply because they were Jews. The grandfather he knew and experienced was a loving man who worked hard and cared for his family.

He remembers the strawberries they would pick in that same

garden. He also remembers that his grandmother always insisted that they should wash these thoroughly before eating. Little did he realise then that the grey dust on the strawberries was the ash from the bodies of those who had perished in the ovens of Auschwitz. The fruit that contained life-giving juices also carried traces of the cruel destruction of life by Rainer's grandfather next door to their home.

For Rainer Höss it was 'hard to explain the guilt, even though there is no reason I should bear any guilt, I still bear it. I carry the guilt with me in my mind. I am ashamed too, of course, for what my family, my grandfather, did to thousands of other families.'[12]

Höss was only able to find some peace after he met with the children and grandchildren of Holocaust victims. They embraced him for enabling their own healing by acknowledging his family's role. He told them his story using a combination of childhood memories and archival material from his grandmother's kist. It was the sight of a swastika emblem on a flag and on his grandfather's uniform that jolted his mind and triggered memories of his childhood, he told them.

Lessons from a pilot workshop on emotional settlement

As founders of the Reimagine Futures Network we came face to face with the reticence to deal with the past on Heritage Day, 24 September 2016. The day coincided with the celebration of the eighty-fifth birthday of the Voortrekker movement. We suggested to the CEO of the Afrikaner Bond, Jan Bosman, that we hold a joint celebration of our heritage by bringing together ten black and ten white young people to reflect on the significance of the day. He agreed, and much time and care went into ensuring a successful process. Lerato Motaung, the CEO of ReimagineSA, would facilitate, and she carefully prepared the workshop in collaboration with Jan Bosman, our host.

The setting of the workshop at Die Eike, the headquarters of the Afrikaner Bond, meant that it was symbolically charged. Here we were at the citadel of what was the seat of power of the apartheid government machinery, the then Broederbond. The walls were bedecked with embossed metal art depicting triumphant and other significant moments in Afrikaner history. Starting with the arrival of Jan van Riebeeck in 1652 and ending with the Union Buildings, the artwork depicted Voortrekker wagon laagers and the Anglo-Boer War concentration camps where 27 000 Boer civilians died alongside 20 000 black people.

The day began on an unpromising note. Only four of the ten white youngsters arrived. A young Afrikaans-speaking black woman from an organisation called Afrikaans Taal en Kultuur joined them. The rest of the young white people who'd been recruited chose to attend the celebrations at the Voortrekker Monument instead. Our host in welcoming us cut an anxious figure standing at the door between his office and the boardroom we would be using for the workshop. He was embarrassed by the no-shows.

Bosman was also intensely uncomfortable about the idea of open conversations about the past to free the present and future. He expressed his concerns. He said that he expected to hear tirades against Afrikaners who were blamed for everything that had gone wrong in the past. He then spent the rest of the day in the entrance hall focusing on the catering arrangements yet listening to every conversation. At times he came to stand at the door of the boardroom to witness the exchanges.

The young people in the room quickly settled down to the introductions and games we'd devised to remember one another's names. The approach we take in the Reimagine workshops is to sit in a circle, as Africans have done for millennia, to promote eye contact and create social proximity. There are no hierarchies in a circle. The opening exercise is to get each person to talk about what they love about South Africa. It's an eye-opener to see how much we have in common. This shared image of the country helps establish a home ground. It helps set the scene for a shared sense of place.

Difficult conversations start with sharing what people fear most about the future. In this instance, we got individuals to jot down their fears anonymously on pieces of paper that were then dropped into a calabash. Discussions centred on the issues raised on these notes retrieved at random from the calabash. Individual comments were solicited, which stimulated intense emotions as opposing views were aired and discussed.

The most controversial discussions were about the artworks on the wall. To some it represented triumph, to others dispossession. Questions of identity, language, power and affirmative action raised the temperature in the room to boiling point. Lerato Motaung is skilled at enabling robust debates on issues without letting matters get out of hand. Yet it became so uncomfortable at times that there was a temptation among us to steer the conversation away from the discomfort. A wise young woman participant pleaded that we 'linger longer' in that place of discomfort and pain to allow it to sink in. Lingering longer is the only way to enable the healing process to emerge.

We then watched a documentary, *A Bloody Miracle*. It debunked the notion that ours was a peaceful transition to democracy. It opened with Chris Hani's assassination in the driveway of his home. It detailed the role of military intelligence in stoking the fires of the civil war that raged in townships and rural areas as ANC and IFP cadres positioned themselves for power in the transition to democracy. This was the conclusion Judge Richard Goldstone had reached after his commission spent months deliberating. It was heavy, emotional stuff.

We were all relieved to adjourn for lunch. Our host treated us to a fabulous braai with all the good things that go with it, including *pap* and *chakalaka*. There is nothing like '*pap en vleis*' to make South Africans feel good about themselves. Easy conversations and social interactions helped ease the tensions of the morning session.

The last discussions focused on reactions to the documentary, and these were also highly charged and emotional. White participants felt judged and condemned by association. Some of the black participants were quick to point out that not much had changed in the areas where they lived. For one of the participants whose home was in Boipatong, in the Vaal Triangle, a scene of one of the massacres of the final years of apartheid, this was the first time he was being 'heard'. Repeatedly he lamented the ongoing poverty and marginalisation of Boipatong.

We ended the day exhausted and relieved that despite the wobbly start we had concluded feeling that we had all voiced our opinions. We all took away much to reflect on. The feedback from the participants, including Bosman, was positive. All wanted to have a second round in a township where they could be exposed to, and celebrate, a place the young white people had never visited. The decision was to do a Heritage Walk in Alexandra in December

2016. Alexandra was chosen rather than Soweto in an effort to move off the beaten path to a road less well travelled.

For us it is clear that the journey to an emotional settlement in our country will be a long and painful one. But its necessity is not in doubt when you consider the responses of these young people. We will need many more such conversations directly and indirectly as the process of healing continues to build a future we can co-own.

DeGruy's concept of vacant self-esteem has resonance for us in post-apartheid South Africa. The behaviour of self-sabotage triggered by vacant self-esteem is evident across the board. Service delivery protests that degenerate too often into a destruction of public property are indicators of our woundedness. The tendency of trade union–supported strikes to descend into violence that destroys the very basis of their livelihoods is an example of self-sabotage behaviour. Student protests that lead to the destruction of public property and education infrastructure speak of a woundedness that is undermining the very future to which these young people aspire.

The widespread abuse of public resources documented in the public protector's 2016 report, 'State of Capture', is an indicator of a total disregard of propriety in public service. The deliberate undermining of the very foundations of our democracy, the rules of public service, the key institutions of our state machinery and the values of the constitution, and the corrupting of so many talented young people, come from a deep sense of disconnection with everything that Ubuntu stands for.

The failure of many in public office, starting with President Zuma, to honour their oath to serve the public good might partly be a reflection of this vacant self-esteem. Why would someone who fought for freedom, or whose relatives sacrificed their lives for freedom, defile the dream of a just society? How can greed by a few be allowed to undermine the aspirations of a people who fought so hard for their freedom? Liberation struggle heroes need to confront this betrayal of their own and other citizens' dreams by the insatiable hunger to reward themselves for the sacrifices they made during the struggle. They need to understand that no amount of wealth and luxury can make up for the deep wounds of the soul that are crying out for healing.

It is critically important to embark on a national programme to heal our society from the traumas of the past before more damage is done. In addition, we need to devote time and resources to address the impact of the ongoing disregard for the majority of citizens by an unaccountable government. It is time to reimagine what a truly free, just society could look like. Reimagining our beloved country in its full glory will enable us to reach across the boundaries of divisions and injustices to forge a shared vision. We need to believe again in unity in diversity in a just, equitable society.

CHAPTER 6

Ubuntu as a healing framework

African wisdom puts human connectedness at the core of social relationships in invoking the notion of Ubuntu. At the heart of Ubuntu is the affirmation of your humanity as predicated on the affirmation by, and of, others. Human community is only possible through mutual respect, support and affirmation. We often boast about our rootedness in Ubuntu as a philosophical standpoint. How can we use this grounding to help heal ourselves as a society?

In traditional African society Ubuntu shapes the conduct of social relationships and underpins the nurture and upbringing of young people to enable them to become proud members of their communities. Exemplary people in traditional African societies are known as *abantu* – people who exude Ubuntu.

Michael Onyebuchi Eze, a Zimbabwean academic based at Cambridge University, refers to Ubuntu thus:

'A person is a person through other people' strikes an affirmation of one's humanity through recognition of an 'other' in his or her uniqueness and difference. It is a demand for a creative inter-subjective formation in which the 'other' becomes a mirror (but only a mirror) for my subjectivity.

This idealism suggests to us that humanity is not imbedded in my person solely as an individual; my humanity is co-substantively bestowed upon the other and me. Humanity is a quality we owe to each other. We create each other and need to sustain this otherness creation. And if we belong to each other, we participate in our creations: we are because you are, and since you are, definitely I am. The 'I am' is not a rigid subject, but a dynamic of self-constitution dependent on this otherness creation of relation and distance.[1]

The values embedded in this understanding of Ubuntu are profound. A better understanding of this philosophy could enrich our approach to our identity as individuals, our relationships to other individuals, our family, our community, the wider society and the world in which we live. Proceeding from the notion that humanity is a quality we owe to each other imposes an inescapable ethical and moral code on our social relationships. It is not an option whether I respect your human dignity, but it is an obligation and condition of my being human.

We could take heart from this Ubuntu grounding to sit together and acknowledge to one another that the wounds and pains of our divided past are undermining our humanity. The future we aspire to is imprisoned by our unacknowledged past. Our inability to affirm our humanity through recognition of the 'other' in their uniqueness and differences makes creating a shared community difficult.

From a very different perspective, Nora Bateson, an artist and thinker, challenges the notion of the 'I' as reflecting 'a singularity that is a semantic, ideological, epistemological, cultural, biological, ecological, evolutionary, epigenetic, gender specific, nationalistic error'.[2] She takes issue with that singularity as doing a great violence and silencing the interdependence that is a more accurate condition of being human. The interconnectedness and interdependence of humanity stretches across boundaries of geography and culture. For instance, a greater awareness of planetary climate changes and our limited resources is a constant reminder of our connectedness.

The whole colonial and apartheid project that privileged people on the basis of skin colour goes against the grain of Ubuntu. To add insult to injury, those who abrogated to themselves privileges over others were strangers who were made to feel at home by the indigenous people whom they later turned against and demeaned and killed. The extended hospitality of the indigenous people, inspired by Ubuntu, opened the door to others whose greed led to kindness being repaid with brutality.

Racial discrimination and oppression go against the very essence of humanity as a quality we owe each other. Racism negates our connectedness as the core of our human nature. And while it denies the humanity of the oppressed it also repudiates that of the oppressor. The oppressor is the mirror of the oppressed; they share an inextricable link through the dynamic of self-construction to which Eze refers. My self-constitution as fully human is dependent on you sustaining your own humanity. The act of oppression effectively breaks the links that enable the dynamic of our co-constitution as human beings. Oppression makes human community impossible.

Ubuntu also provides a way forward in the restitution of our connectedness. Ubuntu's approach to justice is conciliatory, not punitive. But the process of conciliation requires face-to-face encounters to enable the reconnection to occur in a safe and supportive place. In traditional society wrongdoers present themselves supported by close family and people of significance. The wronged party equally comes into such conversations with the support of family and friends. Wrongdoing against one member of the family or clan is regarded in such traditional societies as an insult to the dignity of the rest of the family or clan.

Healing the broken links in our human connectedness requires this coming together to acknowledge what has gone wrong and to ask for forgiveness. Refusing forgiveness in the context of such conversations goes against accepted tradition. It is simply not done. One goes into this process of conciliation confident that there will be closure and on the understanding that a full disclosure will be made.

The Truth and Reconciliation Commission of the mid-1990s started us on a path we should have refined and broadened to create opportunities for us to heal ourselves. The TRC's focus on gross violations of human rights enabled those who had created the ethos for these violations to escape culpability. We should have taken the process of reconciliation beyond the focus of gross violations of human rights. We should have embraced violations of socio-economic rights in our conversations as well.

The fear at the time was that those who relinquished power in the political settlement would not agree to include the violation of socio-economic rights. This was an understandable standpoint by those who knew how difficult it had been to reach a political settlement. They did not want to risk unravelling the deal. Hindsight and distance from the cut and thrust of the transition gives us an opportunity to now tackle what was left unattended.

Dan Bar-On's experience in the conciliation process has found that for healing to occur there needs to be a top-down political process that creates an awareness of social justice, and a bottom-up process motivated by citizens to address psychosocial and inter-personal justice. The TRC was part of the top-down political process. A bottom-up citizen-driven process is urgently needed. ReimagineSA aims to connect, advocate and ignite actions across civil society, business and the public sectors to promote conciliation and achieve an emotional settlement.

We need to create circles of healing at all levels of our society to treat ourselves. Such a process requires listening very attentively to one another. More listening than speaking by all participants is a critical factor if the endeavour is to be successful. This attentiveness would help us learn again to see ourselves in each other and to strengthen the inextricable links between us as human beings. It is this healing process that would address the pent-up anger, frustration and violence that erupts every so often in our society.

Engaging in an emotional settlement through sharing our stories as fellow citizens would put us in a state of mind that opens the way to mutual understanding and affirmation. Healing cannot be sustained unless there is a holistic approach that involves conversations at all levels of society: the home where attitudes are formed and affirmed; the school environment where minds and souls are nurtured into maturity; work places where productivity is undermined by mistrust and prejudiced leadership attitudes; places of worship where spiritual nourishment is impeded by egotism, materialism and suspicion; and public spaces where leaders have lost their vocation to be accountable servants of the people.

Ubuntu is also recognised as an important source of law within the context of strained or broken relationships among individuals or communities and as an aid for providing mutually acceptable remedies in such situations. Ubuntu is the antithesis of vengeance. It places a high value on human life. It is inextricably linked to values that advocate dignity, compassion and humaneness. It encourages a shift from confrontation to mediation and conciliation.

As I have mentioned, Ubuntu favours restorative over retributive justice. It works on sensitising a disputant or a defendant in litigation to the hurtful impact of his or her actions to the other party and encourages changing such conduct rather than punishing the aggressor. It favours civility and civilised dialogue premised on mutual respect and tolerance.

I am confident that Ubuntu would enable us to reimagine ours as a society where our unity in diversity takes on a reality that would not only be celebrated but govern our every engagement. Ubuntu is the balm that can heal our woundedness and enable us to unambiguously identify ourselves as South Africans.

We need to reconnect with our primary common identity as citizens and to celebrate it. We are one of the few countries in the world where citizens do not unselfconsciously self-identify as citizens of their country. We continue to have greater attachments to our secondary identities as whites, blacks, Xhosa, Zulu, Venda, Afrikaners or even Europeans or Westerners. An emotional settlement would make us much more self-assured as South Africans. Our secondary identities would be under no threat in a society where unity in diversity is a lived reality.

I am convinced that healing our wounds will promote a higher consciousness of our common shared humanity. And a higher consciousness of our shared humanity and the richness of our cultural diversity will enable us to wear our common citizenship with greater ease.

Areas of our woundedness crying out for healing

David Whyte, an English poet, reminds us of the critical role of memory in our lives: 'We actually inhabit memory as a living threshold, as a place of choice and volition and imagination, a crossroads where our future diverges according to how we interpret, or perhaps more accurately, how we live the story we have inherited.'[3] Memories cannot be erased. They are embedded in our body, mind and spirit.

Many of us have been wounded in ways that we feel embarrassed to disclose. We need help from those trained in facilitating conversations so that as participants we can tell our stories without feeling judged. This is why religious communities need to be engaged in such a process of healing conversations. Circles of healing are also part of traditional African society to create inclusion and to make everyone feel that they have the same standing as they communicate face to face.

Storytelling is an invaluable tool in the healing process. Again Joy DeGruy's wisdom is apposite and worth repeating: 'Telling our stories can be redemptive. Telling our stories can free us. Story telling is an important part of our education; it strengthens us and builds resilience. It helps us put things in the proper perspective.'4

We would be wise to harness the lessons of experts in sharing our stories in a way that helps us to identify and recognise our strengths. Undoubtedly this would help ease our pathway to healing. Building resilience on our existing strengths is a critical success factor. We would then put our pain and wounds in their proper perspective.

There are key areas of woundedness that need to be addressed in our society. In addition to the core issue of racist exploitation, we need to tackle the impact of struggle politics on the quality of our politics, and the impact of patriarchy on our social relationships.

The impact of struggle politics

The healing process to effect an emotional settlement requires deep introspection by black citizens to acknowledge how their woundedness undermines their ability to assume the responsibilities and rights of citizenship. We have allowed ourselves to accept a narrative of the struggle that reduces us to the status of passive recipients of freedom with the ANC as our liberator. We have, over the last twenty-three years, acquiesced in the erasure of our agency as active participants in the struggle for freedom.

We have become tolerant of the use of this narrative as an excuse for the entitlement to rule by the ANC. Acknowledging and celebrating the very significant role the ANC played in our struggle for freedom does not have to come at the expense of distorting history. We need to heed the demands of students for a more robust approach to African and South African history in our schools and universities.

The impact of Black Consciousness on the struggle for liberation needs to be harnessed to help us find our voice again. We need to draw strength from our success in ditching the 'non-white' label to rename ourselves black and proud. Recalling memories of the surging self-empowerment that enabled us to mobilise ourselves to resist a racist system would bolster us as we assert our rights and discharge our responsibilities against an unaccountable government today. We dare not continue to betray the sacrifices of the generation that led the 1976 uprisings by not listening to the voices of today's generation of young people.

Exile was also a very wounding experience. Those who lived in exile during that brutal period of the struggle for freedom also need to acknowledge the wounds they suffered at the hands of the enemy, as well as the abuse they endured from fellow comrades. The need for healing should cover all these areas. The loss of the anchors of family and familiar neighbourhoods and the sacrifice of one's youth to the struggle has left many wounded. For them, re-rooting in the post-apartheid society has not been easy. There are countless people who disappeared leaving families with gaping holes in their hearts. For these families there has been no resolution.

In his memoir on life in exile, Hugh Macmillan chronicles with great sensitivity the loneliness, pain, alienation, sense of loss, and waste of energy and time that were essential features of life for most exiles for much of the time. Mazisi Kunene captured this poignantly in a poem that Macmillan quotes:

How terrible the fate of a man in exile!
I am a wanderer roaming in foreign
Lands.
I have earned the name of Dingiswayo, 'The exiled one'.

Life in exile stole my youth.
Often I have to salute a low breed of Upstarts.[5]

Many of the returnees and veterans of the struggle continue to endure lives of despair and destitution. They experience abandonment on the margins of society by their own comrades who have betrayed them in favour of power and privilege. All those who continue to live in internal exile need to be considered and heard. They should be able to mourn their losses, be embraced by others in their grief and assisted to find a way forward to lead dignified lives.

We also need to heal from a new form of control that has captured the minds of poor people: namely, the active cultivation of a dependence on government to solve all our problems. As citizens, black and white, we have been complicit in this new form of control and enslavement by not raising the alarm loudly enough and consistently. Many of us have turned a blind eye so that we can enjoy the patronage that flows from corrupt deals in a corrupt state.

Black people also need to confront the deeper psychosocial reasons for their continuing tolerance of the ANC's abuse of power. To reiterate: black people, having endured the humiliation of deep-seated stereotypical attitudes and practices, are afraid of being seen to be criticising fellow black people in leadership positions, lest this fuels attacks by racists. Solidarity takes the form of silence in the face of wrongdoing by people who should be held accountable. Many believe that speaking out as a black person against corruption and incompetence would be seen as conceding to racist stereotypes of black people's inability to lead.

The lessons of history about this 'silence' abound on our continent and elsewhere. 'A society haunted by fears of the past and fears of the present is easy prey for opportunistic political leaders,' says Dan Bar-On.[6] In many instances, post-colonial and former liberation movement leaders have kept themselves in power by engendering fear among citizens. Fear of former colonials returning as neo-colonials is reason for a life presidency to stand guard over a hard-won freedom. Fear of racists in whatever guise – 'clever blacks' or agents of imperialists – reversing the gains of freedom in post-apartheid South Africa is reason enough for continuing to vote for an unaccountable former liberation party. If all else fails, then fear of being disappeared or your reputation being ruined by false accusations is often enough to silence the dissenting citizen's voice.

Then there is the fear of fulfilling an ever-present stereotypical threat that as a black person you might fail and prove the racists right.[7] Add to this, as I have said, the fear of betraying solidarity by exposing corrupt leaders who happen to be black, and you have the black citizen's dilemma. The threat of conforming to a racist stereotype is a fear in many black people. They dare not do anything or say anything that will confirm to racists that they are incompetent, ignorant, dishonest and irresponsible. This type of threat undermines relationships of trust essential for accountability in democratic politics.

We also need to systematically examine and heal the institutional cultures of our educational institutions – pre-schools, schools, universities and colleges – to root out any remnants of racism, sexism and other discriminatory abuse. The outbursts of racist and sexist remarks or actions in our education system need to be addressed as and when they occur if we are to eliminate the underlying prejudices embedded in our diverse cultures. We should not behave like victims, but as shapers of a new future.

We have failed to set the tone of what a non-racial African society should be like – a society in which all matters African are the mainstream in teaching and learning and in cultural endeavours, be they philosophy, language or artistic expressions. Once more I ask: how can we still have schools that punish learners for speaking their mother tongue twenty-three years into our democracy?

African culture's relegation to a minority culture is enabled by our lack of understanding of its strengths and relevance in a society built on human rights. Self-proclaimed liberals or Westerners, as some of them prefer to identify themselves, tend to interpret Ubuntu as only espousing collectivism. They completely miss the celebration of the unique attributes individuals bring to the collective to enrich and strengthen the common good.

Individuality is not only celebrated in African culture, but it is nurtured and reinforced. Praise songs in all African languages identify and amplify the unique attributes of the person being honoured. The clan and the family are the nest within which the individual is situated. A complementarity is at work to recognise the individuality of a person in the strengths of their relationships within the family and wider society.

So-called Western philosophy that crowns the individual as sovereign and autonomous not only disregards the central tenant of Ubuntu – 'I am because you are' – but also diminishes any accountability of the individual to the wider public. In other words, it does not take into account the benefits and privileges that an individual may enjoy that resulted from the violation of the rights of others. In South Africa, the people who are proponents of this form of liberalism are beneficiaries of one of the most successful affirmative action programmes in favour of white people ever implemented in history. The political settlement process to which we agreed entrenched these benefits. An emotional settlement would give us an opportunity to explore these viewpoints so that we can shape a democratic culture aligned to our human rights and the values of Ubuntu.

Building a genuinely non-racial society where the equality of citizens is not just espoused but enacted in everyday life requires acknowledgement of the accrued benefits and privileges of our divided past. Such acknowledgement would enable us to reach an agreement on how to work together to create a country in which all would have access to the resources that have been the exclusive preserve of some. Healing the wounds of the humiliation of poverty in the midst of plenty would unleash the diversity of talents in our society and enlarge the pool of those actively contributing to our greater prosperity.

Gareth van Onselen, a political commentator and former DA official, expressed serious concerns about Mmusi Maimane's injunctions to the DA to set targets at all levels of the party to ensure that candidates for public office reflect the diversity of our society. Maimane is determined to lead a transformed DA into the 2019 general elections. Van Onselen's concerns are that 'racial engineering, whether mild or intense, justified or abhorrent, is highly complex ideological business. Certainly it presents a series of serious challenges for the DA, ostensibly a liberal party, which has thus far managed to resist the ubiquitous nationalistic drive towards manufactured demographic representivity. The dangers of embracing that drive are enormous.'[8]

How can you successfully operate in South Africa as a party representing citizens who are a black majority without taking steps to correct the legacy of exclusion of black people from parliamentary representation and leadership opportunities for so many hundreds of years? How can the DA break the mould of its traditional white male leadership and present a more non-racial alternative? Does Van Onselen acknowledge that it is this legacy of exclusion that has 'manufactured the demographic realities' of the traditional DA leadership that Maimane seeks to address?

Van Onselen's insistence that targets are quotas prevents him from accepting that simply following the rules of 'fairness and equal opportunities' in a society that has yet to redress the disabling of the competitiveness of black people is bound to perpetuate the current white male dominance in leadership positions. All high-performing businesses and institutions the world over set targets to guide them towards attaining their goals. Why is it wrong in our unequal society to set targets to achieve the equality that has eluded us over the last two decades? Healing the wounds of our engineered inequality needs a major attitudinal shift on these issues.

Similarly, religious organisations need to be challenged to halt the further wounding of people suffering social pain. The multitudes of poor desperate people flocking to 'prosperity churches' in search of material success need to confront the vacant self-esteem within themselves. Poor black people need to be assisted to stop being victims of pastors who extract the little they have to enrich themselves. Most of these pastors are fabulously wealthy.

The animist approach to life has pushed people back into fatalistic approaches to life. People seem to place their lives and futures in the hands of those claiming to have the answer to all life's problems. The acceptance of the deaths of seventy-four South African worshippers in the collapse of the Synagogue Church of

All Nations in Lagos, Nigeria, in 2014 demonstrated the lengths to which our fellow citizens are prepared to go in search of supernatural redemptive power.

Healing our wounds as black and white citizens is critical to the emergence of trusting relationships and a shared sense of our common humanity. Let me say it again: we need to heal ourselves to enable the re-establishment of links broken by our painful past, links with our souls, our families and our fellow citizens. We need to recommit to working together to rebuild our country. Unity in diversity is only possible if all parties do the work of preparing themselves to become proud citizens of a reimagined country.

The impact of patriarchy

We also need to address the wounds of the patriarchal system that is so dominant in our society. Patriarchy runs in the veins of all the cultures of our society and, as a result, male dominance continues to wreak havoc in relationships between men and women. The constitutional requirement of gender equality has yet to find expression in our homes, places of work, schools and religious organisations.

Hierarchical relationships frame the institutional cultures of a significant majority. The good progress made in women's representation in public life – parliament, government, the public service, the private sector and the professions – has not been accompanied by the eradication of attitudes and practices that undermine women at many levels.

The demands of masculinity with its celebration of the alpha male are anchored by *power* and *control*. Real men have money and control over its use, according to this world view. They occupy leadership positions in public life, flaunt their sexual prowess, are hardy and boast intellectual superiority.[9] This dominant masculinity model operates on a competitive 'winner takes all' approach to power that undermines those men defined as losers. In short, the alpha-male dominance is sustained by destabilising other males.

But what are the alternative masculinities on which young men can model themselves? Gender equality is at the heart of our constitutional democratic values, yet we still privilege and celebrate the model of the alpha male. The dissonance between what our constitution calls for and what we practise in reality can only produce conflict and violence.

The dominant masculinity model operates through the subjugation of others. Women and children become collateral damage when men defined as losers in this model take out their frustration on those closest to them who are perceived as weaker than them. Those dominated and abused become dominant abusers as well.

Think of young men who opt for a different approach and are gentle, communicative, empathetic and caring people who show their emotions, and enjoy teamwork, collaboration and partnerships, rather than participate in a competitive dog-eat-dog attitude. Would we encourage them and hold them up as positive role models? Or would we join those who call them wimps, moffies and sissies? How do we respond when they are ridiculed? Do we challenge those ridiculing them or do we join the fray? Healing our fear of 'weakness' that defines 'strength' as male dominance is critical to challenging abusive intimate relationships.

Why are we so tolerant of displays of masculinity that celebrate ostentatious consumption and risky behaviours such as drag racing, binge drinking and sex parties? The mushrooming of 'adult shops' reflects the narcissistic focus that drives men and women to seek instantaneous satisfaction in sexual fantasies. So-called sex workers are also a product of an alpha-male society that celebrates men's insatiable sexual urges by 'allowing' these women to indulge them.

The growing human trafficking of young women and children is a new form of slavery in our society and our world. How do we reconcile respect for human rights with the sale of human bodies to satisfy the urges of the men who have money and power? Why don't we develop a society in which women can create and sustain honourable livelihoods without the indignity of selling their bodies?

Even more complex are the masculinities of transgender and gay men. How comfortable are we with affirming the manhood of those whose sexual preferences and expressions challenge the traditional view of what a man is or is not? Are we able to affirm them as real men who deserve the same respect as all others?

Are we willing to socialise our children to acknowledge the diversity of masculinities as equally valid in our society? Are our institutions of learning creating enough safe places for conversations about gender diversities? What provisions are we making for the expression of alternative masculinities in the arts, sports and other aspects of our social institutions?

Women as mothers, aunts, grandmothers, wives, sisters and community members also have to confront their own fears, hopes and prejudices about challenging the traditional dominant male model. To what extent are we as women open to nurturing and affirming our sons and grandsons who may display non-traditional male characteristics? Are we willing to encourage them and advocate openly for their rights?

Women leaders have to step forward and set the tone of healing conversations about gender equality and the importance of the non-dominant male. We need to have open conversations about the incompatibility of the dominant masculinity model with the social justice values of our constitution and the core values of Ubuntu. A non-racial, non-sexist, egalitarian value system cannot be embedded in a society that operates according to a patriarchy characterised by command and control.

The wounds of gender inequity are visible and palpable in our high statistics of gender-based violence (GBV). Gender Links, an NGO formed in 2001 to tackle this scourge in the Southern African Development Community, or SADC, region, found in its research[10] that 77 per cent of women in Limpopo province, 51 per cent of women in Gauteng, 45 per cent of women in the Western Cape and 36 per cent of women in KwaZulu-Natal have experienced some form of violence (emotional, economic, physical or sexual) in their lifetime, both within and outside intimate relationships.

The research found a higher proportion of men in Gauteng (76 per cent) and KwaZulu-Natal (41 per cent) admitted to perpetrating violence against women, while a slightly lower proportion of men – compared to the proportion of women reporting GBV – said they perpetrated GBV in Limpopo (48 per cent) and Western Cape (35 per cent). 'Comparing what women say they experience to what men say they do confirm that GBV is a reality in South Africa,' Gender Links concluded.[11]

According to the research, most of the violence reported occurred within women and men's private lives, with 51 per cent of women in Gauteng, 51 per cent in Limpopo, 44 per cent in the Western

Cape and 29 per cent in KwaZulu-Natal reporting having experienced intimate partner violence. 'The low prevalence of GBV reported by women in KwaZulu-Natal is indicative of an even bigger problem that women may not be openly disclosing their experiences,' Gender Links reported.

Women are also vulnerable to violence in public life, the research found, with 12 per cent of women in Gauteng, 6 per cent in the Western Cape, 5 per cent in Limpopo and 5 per cent in KwaZulu-Natal reporting having experienced non-partner rape. 'The proportion of men reporting rape perpetration in the four provinces is significantly higher than the proportion of women reporting the experience,' according to Gender Links. 'In Gauteng, 31 per cent of men admitted to having raped a woman at least once in their lifetime.'

Over half (59 per cent) of the women in Limpopo, 5 per cent in KwaZulu-Natal, 5 per cent in the Western Cape and slightly less than 3 per cent in Gauteng who had ever worked reported having been sexually harassed. 'They disclosed that a man either hinted or threatened that they would lose their job if they did not have sex with him; or they would have to have sex with him in order to get a job,' reported Gender Links. Almost two-thirds of women in Limpopo, 2 per cent in KwaZulu-Natal, and just over 1 per cent in Gauteng and the Western Cape who had attended school said they had experienced sexual harassment at school.

We need deep conversations about how we are to face the demon of male dominance that is driving gender-based violence and consequently hurting so many women and children. Male dominance and violent relationships between men and women, like all other forms of oppression, hurt the perpetrators as well. Men who are abusers are often also victims of earlier domestic and other forms of violence.

Men feeling vulnerable due to poverty and unemployment often struggle with a sense of worthlessness. They are supposed to be providers and protectors of their families, yet see themselves as failures in this regard. Black men, being over-represented among the poor and unemployed, tend to also be over-represented among abusers. It is noteworthy that Limpopo, one of the two poorest provinces, has the highest reported statistics of GBV.

We can no longer continue to run ineffectual campaigns such as 16 Days of Activism Against Gender-Based Violence, which has been propagated by Gender Links since 2001. We need to work together as citizens to deal with the root causes of the violence. Violence is the 'language' of those feeling disempowered, and often sets off a vicious cycle.

We need to commit ourselves to tackling this scourge of gender-based violence and free women and children from its devastating consequences. Ubuntu values need to be embedded in our domestic relationships so boys and girls can grow up with self-respect and respect for others. Parents need to engage in healing conversations to make their relationships whole so they can show respect for each other and create supportive homes.

South Africa is paying an exorbitant price for the appalling levels of gender-based violence. The persistence of high levels of new infections of HIV/AIDS among fifteen- to thirty-year-old women is a major concern. These new infections are often a result of abusive transactional sexual relationships in which these women are trapped. Their poor socio-economic status makes them dependent on older abusive men who refuse to use condoms. Patriarchal attitudes perpetuate men's sense of entitlement to women's bodies. Such attitudes contradict the values of our shared humanity. Mutual respect and reverence for the human body are the foundation stones of Ubuntu.

We need to mobilise men and women to become advocates of gender equality so that we can end gender-based violence. We need to mobilise traditional leaders and those involved in male and female initiation ceremonies to reinforce the values of respect for human dignity as central to being mature men and women. As I have said, human dignity is a core value that is enshrined in both Ubuntu and our constitution.

Citizenship in a healed society would become a badge of honour worn with pride. Citizens would be better able to assume the responsibilities of ensuring the accountable and responsive conduct of leaders in both the public and private sectors as an expression of passion and love of country.

Tackling the unfinished business of socio-economic restructuring is a shared responsibility that will enable more mutually trusting human communities across our country. Human dignity and trusting relationships are prerequisites to unleashing the talents and energies of all fellow citizens to contribute to the country of our dreams. Trusting relationships and deep empathy would lay the basis for the transactional element of the emotional settlement. The unleashing of talent to energise our economic, social and political institutions is essential if we are to enjoy a prosperous and just democracy.

CHAPTER 7

Rebuilding our society

Without doubt an emotional settlement is a critical success factor if we are to transcend seeing ourselves as black and white. A healed society would be one where citizens identify themselves as South Africans first and foremost. A common shared identity, as fellow citizens, would enable us to develop the solidarity that is critical to success in tackling the legacy of structural poverty, unemployment and inequality as an injury to our common humanity.

The shift from storytelling to the identification of commonalities that might serve as ways to envision a future that can be shared by all citizens would represent a transition from the emotional issues that obsess us to a resolution, a settlement. Settlements belong in the realm of transactional engagements: they usher in inter-personal and social justice. The negotiations leading to our political settlement were focused on agreeing to a transactional arrangement that enabled power to move from the minority to the majority.

An emotional settlement would only be sustainable if the transactional element was agreed to by a broad base of stakeholders. Their common purpose would be in the interests of the public good. Such a deal would unlock the talents and energies of all citizens to effect the restructuring of our socio-economic system into one that is inclusive of all citizens. Greater trust would evolve to make productivity a shared interest between workers and managers, shareholders and employees, senior and low-level workers, and unionised and non-unionised workers.

Such a fundamental structural transformation would become a national strategic imperative to boost socio-economic development that would benefit everyone. An emotional settlement would help us refrain from using language that is unhelpful such as 'helping the under-privileged, the less fortunate or the previously disadvantaged'.

Poverty and unemployment are not matters of fortune or misfortune. They are fundamental matters of injustice that call upon all citizens to right what is wrong. Successful restructuring is possible when we, the citizens, embrace the uprooting of poverty and unemployment because they are an affront to the dignity of our fellow citizens and undermine our common humanity. An affront to the dignity of one is an affront to our human community.

Legislative requirements and the enforcement of labour compliance with redistributive policies such as black economic empowerment (BEE) alone have not been, and will not be, sufficient. Much more is needed to successfully meet the challenges we face to consign poverty, unemployment and inequalities to the waste bin. BEE incentivises and perpetuates the categorisation of South Africans using apartheid tools to the detriment of promoting a common identity. It has spawned a patronage system not dissimilar to that of the apartheid era that enriches some at the expense of the majority. BEE is also used to legitimise corruption and nepotism.

The reality is that black people as a majority of the population would benefit the most from a robust system of governance and socio-economic development that strategically focused on redressing injustices and promoting prosperity for all. Such an approach would embrace the eradication of poverty and unemployment as an essential building block for a country committed to inclusive prosperity. Socio-economic restructuring needs to have as its endgame stewardship of the economy by the majority.

What are the facts?

Thomas Piketty, a French economist, gave us stark figures in his 2015 Nelson Mandela Annual Lecture:

> Just to take an example, there are other countries in the world, unfortunately, where you have very high unemployment – Spain or Greece, where you also have a 25% rate of unemployment – and you don't have that level of income inequality. You still have 30%–35% of total income to the top 10% as compared to 60%–65% in South Africa.
>
> So even if the data is not perfect, I think it's very clear that the extreme level of inequality we have in South Africa is much more than just unemployment. It has to do, certainly, with the legacy of apartheid. In particular, it is striking to see what is really different in South Africa compared to other countries is the top 10% share – if you take the top 1% share it is not so different from the US today, but if you take the top 10% share, then it's really higher in South Africa.
>
> So this really suggests that you have a relatively large group

in the country, around 10%, which is very far away from the rest of the population. Of course, this group historically has been predominantly, almost exclusively, white. Even today if you look at the data, especially within the top 1%–5%, it will be up to 80% white, so things have changed a little bit, but we are still very much with this same structure of racial inequality that we used to have. So now how can we make progress?[1]

This is the question we cannot escape.

Our economy has ground to a halt. There is now overwhelming evidence that only major structural transformation can get us out of our predicament. Inequality is expensive for all, rich and poor, declared Richard Wilkinson and Kate Pickett in their appropriately titled book *The Spirit Level: Why Equality is Better for Everyone.*[2] Building a society and institutions that can endure beyond our lifetimes requires the use of a 'spirit level' to ensure proper alignments in our social structures. We can do no better than learn from master builders across the ages who relied on the spirit level to secure their buildings. We need to level out the inequalities in our society to strengthen the foundations of our beloved country.

Land restitution and reform remains a major economic and emotive issue in our unfinished transformation. Black people cannot build effective capital without owning property, including the important matter of land ownership. Thomas Piketty's observation about our poor performance in addressing the land question challenges us to recommit to tackling this as a matter of urgency:

> [The] effective right which I want to stress is the right to access to property. That is probably one of the more complicated

rights, because it involves very difficult and sensitive issues, including land reform. Let me just say that if we take a broad international historical perspective, we see in many countries, in history, much more ambitious land reforms than what we have seen in South Africa since the end of apartheid.

I think it's fair to say that black economic empowerment (BEE) strategies, which were mostly based on voluntary market transactions,... were not that successful in spreading the wealth and limiting the extreme concentration of wealth from which we start in South Africa. So I think we need to think again about more ambitious land reform.[3]

It is encouraging to see that the International Monetary Fund (IMF) is now of the view that sustainable development and economic growth rates are undermined by inequality among citizens. The stewardship of the economy by the black majority is the only guarantor of sustainable socio-economic development.

David Lipton, the first deputy managing director of the IMF, had tough advice for South Africans in his July 2016 speech at the Wits Business School. He observed that our stagnant economy needs radical action to stimulate inclusive sustainable growth: 'A huge part of the labour force is left on the outside looking in, undereducated and with no prospects for advancement. The formal economy is not absorbing them, nor are they able to strike out on their own.'[4]

Lipton attributes this exclusion to crucial structural issues. Large businesses, banks and unionised labour maintain high barriers against their potential competitors: small and medium enterprises, as well as the unemployed. The four big banks were singled out as examples of 'privileged market players' supported by government regulations that suppress innovation and raise the cost of capital for entrepreneurs and individual borrowers.

Living in the US from 2000 to 2004 opened my eyes to the high transaction costs we incur in our banking system. I enjoyed low-cost banking with zero charges for ATM withdrawals from my bank in the US. This contrasts starkly with South African practices of paying to deposit money. We pay for withdrawing cash from an ATM belonging to our own bank. We pay for keeping our money in savings accounts. So why are we surprised by a low level of banking and an underdeveloped savings culture?

Lipton also raised concerns about anti-competitive conduct in many other industries often reinforced by government regulations that entrench vested interests. The IMF's conclusion is clear. It is only fundamental structural reforms that will boost employment – particularly for young people – reduce inequality and promote economic inclusion.

Two key industries that are undermining inclusive economic growth through their 'privileged market' practices are the financial services and cellular phone and data companies. High bank charges and barriers to access finance make the cost of doing business prohibitive especially for first-time entrants into the business world. The hoops through which young black entrants into the business world must jump are a disincentive to entrepreneurship. Who you know seems to be more important than the quality of your business proposition when it comes to the cost of capital. This undermines small- and medium-enterprise development, which is the driver of economic growth in most countries.

The digital divide is widening in our society due to high connectivity costs. Airtime pre-payment, used mainly by poor and young people, is more expensive than contract rates for higher-end customers. The Independent Communications Authority of South Africa seems to have finally woken up to its responsibilities after a public outcry over data costs. Data prices in our country are much higher than those in other countries on the continent and in the world. While one gigabyte of data costs R11 in India, R22 in Nigeria and R32 in Namibia, South Africans are paying a whopping R150 per gigabyte. To add insult to injury, South African cellular companies offer lower costs to other African countries compared to the very high costs locally. Why has this been allowed to happen? Are there conflicts of interest involved in the regulatory environment or is it just neglect? We are shooting ourselves in the foot and need to come down hard on these 'privileged market' practices.

The February 2016 World Bank report titled 'South Africa economic update: Promoting faster growth and poverty alleviation through competition' suggests that we could lift 200 000 people out of poverty by reducing retail and professional service prices through ending cartels that operate in key sectors of our economy. Our Competition Commission needs to improve its capacity to detect anti-competitive acts and use much stronger deterrents than a fine of 9 per cent of profits. Elsewhere this is 25 per cent and acts as a disincentive. Regulations also need to be strengthened for professional services. Estimated savings for companies could amount to between $1.4 and $1.6 billion, adding almost half a per cent to gross domestic product (GDP). Advocacy by citizens and civil society groups can prevent potential abusers flying under the radar.[5]

The IMF has over the last two years also focused on the importance of the greater participation of women in the economy to enhance socio-economic growth and sustainability. A study conducted in 2013 by women economists at the IMF examined the growth prospects of several countries if they were to equalise the economic participation of men and women. It concluded that parity in male and female participation in the labour force would add 5 per cent to GDP growth in the US, 9 per cent in Japan, 12 per cent in the United Arab Emirates and 34 per cent in Egypt.[6]

In addition, the study demonstrated that better opportunities for women to earn and control income could contribute to broader economic development in developing countries. Improvements would result in areas such as higher levels of school enrolment of girls and their success in preparing themselves for skills development and participation in the economy. Equal access to finance and trading would also raise the productivity of female-owned enterprises. It stands to reason that a wider pool of talent in any given society enhances growth prospects.

A 2015 McKinsey Global Institute (MGI) report confirmed that gender 'inequality is not only a pressing moral and social issue but also a critical economic challenge. If women – who account for half the world's working-age population – do not achieve their full economic potential, the global economy will suffer.' The MGI report, titled 'The power of parity: How advancing women's equality can add $12 trillion to global growth', focused on 'the economic implications of lack of parity between men and women'.[7]

The report concluded that a 'best in region' scenario, in which all countries match the rate of advancement of the fastest-improving country in their region, could add as much as $12 trillion, or 11 per cent, to global annual GDP by 2025. In a 'full-potential' scenario in which women play an identical role in labour markets to that of men, as much as $28 trillion, or 26 per cent, could be added to global annual GDP by 2025. MGI's full-potential estimate was about double the average estimate of other recent studies, because they had taken a more comprehensive view of gender inequality in the workplace. The study estimated that sub-Saharan Africa could benefit by 12 per cent growth in its GDP by 2025 from gender parity in the workplace.

The question for us is how are we to undertake socio-economic restructuring in the light of what we know works in other societies similar to ours? How are we to tackle the bottlenecks in our society? How do we build on the strong pillars already present to redesign our country into the one promised at the birth of our democracy in 1994?

What are the strategic pathways to socio-economic restructuring?

We need to agree that investing in restructuring our society is a shared responsibility for citizens in both the private sector and the public sector. We need to approach the process as an essential steppingstone to building our reimagined country. As I have emphasised, the eradication of poverty, and tackling unemployment and inequality are critical in uniting our society in its diversity. Only when all citizens have a vested interest in growing our economy and sharing the results of a successful democratic and prosperous society can we sustain our gains.

We need to heed the lessons of Germany after the fall of the Berlin Wall in 1989. The reunification of Germany would not have been as successful without the willingness of all Germans to invest in achieving a unified nation. They had talks – similar to my envisaged emotional settlement – about reconstructing a united Germany after the traumas of two world wars and the separation caused by the Berlin Wall.

It was thanks to the leadership of former chancellor Helmut Kohl, who persuaded his compatriots that an unequal Germany could not sustain unity, that Germany is where it is today. Equalising East and West required a long-term solidarity fund. Contributions to the fund had to come from additional taxes and levies from those living in the wealthier West German states.

The focus of the solidarity fund was on investments in education and training, and enhancing the competitiveness of enterprises of the former East Germany. In addition, attention was paid to upgrading the social and physical infrastructure and to providing social welfare payments comparable to those in West Germany. The Organisation for Economic Co-operation and Development estimated that the cost of the solidarity fund to the German economy was about 5 per cent of GDP per annum.

The solidarity fund will continue until 2019 to ensure that all long-term structural problems are adequately addressed. Germany's economy is today the strongest in the European Union. That a former East German woman, Angela Merkel, currently ably leads Germany is a powerful symbol of the success reaped from investment in equality. Clearly this investment has bettered conditions for all Germans in the united country.

We need open, honest conversations about how we are to fund our own socio-economic restructuring process to suit our circumstances. Some may argue that Germany is a more homogenous society making a consensus on a solidarity fund easier to reach. It is my view that the commitment and execution of the emotional settlement process described above – through both a top-down political process, as well as a bottom-up one – is required. Such a combination would enable us to connect across our angry divides and help us appreciate one another as fellow citizens.

It is also now clear that by failing to tackle fundamental socio-economic restructuring our economy has ground to a halt. The anger of those excluded from what little socio-economic development there has been is boiling over in public violence. Witness here the #FeesMustFall movement, and the burning of schools in Vuyani in Limpopo. This is too high a price for us to pay. Inequality and huge unemployment levels undermine our collective success, as the IMF and other analysts point out. We need to take the plunge and commit to long-term investments to kick-start a shared, sustainable prosperity.

We need to set up a Rebuilding South Africa Fund to be managed as a dedicated resource to finance the restructuring of our society. As I have stated, this rebuilt society would be one in which all citizens enjoy human dignity and equal access to resources to develop themselves and contribute to our common wealth. Much of the financing for the fund could become available immediately by redirecting existing public monies that are not applied efficiently and effectively. The following steps are essential:

Firstly, an emotionally settled society would have the courage to stop the corruption that is stealing resources. This would allow for the socio-economic needs of the poor to be addressed. At least R90 billion is estimated by the auditor general to be lost every year to corruption in the public sector without including the losses never revealed by the state-owned enterprises. The 2015/16 audit tells us that there has been an 80 per cent increase in irregular expenditure to R46 billion. Even if we could claw back half of it in 2017, we would have enough money to start the restructuring process.

The chief procurement officer in the Treasury estimates that between 30 and 40 per cent of the annual government procurement budget of R600 billion (2016) is lost to wastage, maladministration and corruption. That is a staggering amount of tax money that could address all the major urgent problems such as free quality education and the recapitalisation of education and training, including enhancing research capacity.

Corruption is the most expensive self-sabotage culture any nation can inflict on itself. It is not only a tax on poor people who are denied essential basic services, but a powerfully disruptive force to investment in sustainable human and intellectual capital critical to propelling high economic growth rates. There should be no place in our public service for saboteurs.

Secondly, the illicit capital outflows (through transfer and mispricing by multinational companies and organised crime), estimated at R420 billion over the last almost forty years,[8] could have done wonders in setting us up as a modern prosperous economy. A high-level panel on illicit cash flows from Africa headed by former president Thabo Mbeki estimated that Africa loses $60 billion annually. It is reasonable to suggest that South Africa, as the most advanced economy, contributes a large proportion of these outflows.

The people behind these illicit flows would probably argue that they are simply securing the future of their children and grandchildren in the face of a corrupt government. Which is why an emotional settlement is necessary, as it would convince the elite that they should rather eradicate corruption than illegally relocate their wealth. Leaders in the private sector cannot pick and choose what activities to be involved in without coming across as freeloaders preying on the efforts of the well intentioned to the detriment of the long-term interests of all.

Thirdly, abolishing the wasteful non-performing Sector Education and Training Authorities (SETAs), which do little to develop skills training, would release no less than R15 billion per year. Private and public sector entities should have skills training as part of their normal business operations as happens in other countries, notably Germany's on-the-job training models.

Partnerships between employers, especially those in the private sector, with further education and training colleges would greatly enhance the quality of training and skills development directly matched to industry's needs. On-the-job training agreed to as part of an employee/employer partnership would also build trust between all players to enhance productivity and grow our economy.

We need to identify priorities for action and start with those areas likely to yield the biggest returns and unlock further opportunities. The following suggest themselves:

- education transformation, including second-chance education and training for the estimated four million unemployed youth; and
- urban renewal programmes.

In the next chapters I will examine key areas of restructuring essential to rebuilding the South Africa we dare to reimagine.

CHAPTER 8

Reimagined education and skills training

A reimagined South Africa in a redesigned education and training system would be one that stimulates, identifies, nurtures and promotes the talents of all the children and young people. Human capital and intellectual capital are the essential ingredients of a competitive, sustainable, inclusive socio-economic development process. We have a great opportunity to reignite our stagnant economy by opening access to education and training. Provided we redevelop these disciplines. Countries as varied as Singapore, Finland, South Korea, Ireland and Rwanda have demonstrated the wisdom of investing in high-quality education and training for all.

Finland rose from being the poorest in the Scandinavian region, with an economy dependent on paper and pulp, to becoming a technology and innovation giant. In fact it has outshone its peers over the last few decades. It deliberately invested in quality education and created incentives for creativity and innovation. South

Korea has become an extremely competitive industrial country after the traumatic Korean War by investing in a high-quality, flexible education and training system. Rwanda has shown dramatic growth and development by investing in innovative high-quality education and training in the aftermath of the 1994 genocide that ripped apart the country's heart and soul. It is repositioning itself as the 'Switzerland' of Africa.

The 'private and social' return on investing in education has proven to be singularly impressive. Private returns are higher and easier to calculate than social returns. The higher the level of education, the higher the private return. Internationally, researchers are reporting similar findings. Claudio E. Montenegro and Harry Patrinos found that:

- The returns to schooling are 10 per cent per year of schooling;
- The returns to schooling are higher for women than for men;
- The returns to tertiary education are higher than the returns to primary or secondary schooling; and
- There is a decreasing pattern over time, meaning that as schooling levels rise, the returns tend to decline, but only modestly.[1]

In a blog for the World Bank, Patrinos talks about Alexandria Valerio's paper titled 'The skills payoff in low and middle income countries', which looked at private returns to investments in schooling in eight countries (Armenia, Bolivia, Colombia, Georgia, Ghana, Kenya, Ukraine and Vietnam). Her findings were based on data reflecting cognitive and non-cognitive skills:

- There are positive and significant wage benefits associated with a year of schooling;
- Better cognitive skills yield significant pay-offs; and
- Several socio-emotional skills matter for earnings, those types of skills are rewarded differently in different countries.[2]

In addition, Valerio measured the returns to investments in specific job market skills. She found that computer skills had the highest pay-off in all the countries over and above education and other skills.

Without a doubt we need to radically transform our severely under-performing education and training system. Free education from pre-school to higher education is not only affordable, but is also the best investment we can make to equalise opportunities for every child and thereby transform our society's fortunes.

The education budget at 17.5 per cent of government expenditure is an indicator of the government's commitment to education, but the expenditure is inefficient and ineffective. In his 2017 budget speech, the minister of finance allocated R240 billion to basic education for R2017/18. Aside from our public investment in education, many parents have demonstrated their commitment to investing in the education of their children. The richest citizens pay between R142 000 and R253 000 per year to get their children into boarding schools such as Herschel Girls School in Cape Town or the expensive Hilton College in KwaZulu-Natal.

At university level, government subsidies reduce the level of fees. For instance, at an expensive university such as UCT, bachelor of science and engineering degrees can be subsidised by between R80 000 and R95 000 for tuition and residence. At the less expensive

University of North West the fee is about R68 000. We need to migrate to full-cost financial aid for all needy students and eventually provide free high-quality education for all children from Grade R to tertiary level. Taking the burden of financial insecurity off the minds of young people would also enhance their performance.

The repayment to society for free education could be done through a form of 'national service'. For instance, post-graduates could 'refund' their fees by doing national service in teaching, health sciences and other areas of public service at local government, provincial and national levels. This would be compulsory for everyone. Such national service, like the Peace Corps in the US founded in 1961 under President J.F. Kennedy, would provide essential life-changing experiences that would stand young people in good stead in their professional lives.

We also need to consider the distressing disruptions to teaching and learning in our tertiary education sector. A vocal minority of young people has resorted to violence and the destruction of public property due to their perception that their voices are only heard if they indulge in violent protest. They remind us of the unfinished business that Es'kia Mphahlele, in a graduation address at the University of the Witwatersrand, urged us to pay attention to as far back as 1995:

> In the heat and crush, push and shove, urgency, preoccupations, panic and heartburn of the times, it is easy to lose sight of the essence of the dramatic events and issues that have come to the forefront of our consciousness these days around tertiary institutions. We are also afraid of coming to terms with the burden of our history, which bedevils the education crisis we

are in. This crisis, we observe, brings out the ugliest in us as academics, students, workers and administrators, and often belies the best we can bring to the hammer and anvil on which we are currently trying to reshape the present into the future.'[3]

We need to learn the lessons of our own history. The 1976 student uprisings demonstrated the power of young people to risk all for the ideal of high-quality education free of the ideological burden that sought to perpetuate their dehumanisation and inferior status. Between 1995 and 2000 tertiary education student protests were about aligning the tertiary institutions with our political settlement and the demand for fundamental transformation at the national level.

We must acknowledge that our education system today, at both the basic and tertiary levels, has failed to rise to the historical opportunities. Where it should be a fountain of talent development and a nurturing ground for ideas, it is, instead, a system of contention. Our distress at the violence and destruction of public property is understandable, but it stands in stark contrast to our failure to express outrage at the continuing destruction of talent and hope in successive generations. What nation can normalise the theft of hope from so many of its young? Twenty-three years after our political settlement, children still face high infant and child mortality rates in a middle-income country.

In addition, 50 per cent of our children drop out of school. Of those who don't and enter our tertiary sector, 50 per cent eventually drop out. Where is our outrage at the pain of the more than four million young people who are unemployed and walking our streets and villages? Where is our outrage at the millions who find solace from humiliation and despair in substance abuse? Where is the outrage against this monumental destruction of the seed of our future by our education and training system?

A prerequisite for transformation in education is the assumption that every child has unique gifts to be nurtured. As we rebuild our society according to the values of Ubuntu we will focus on human dignity and self-respect, empathy and collaboration. Embedding civic education in the teaching of our children and young people is critical to the success of our constitutional democracy.

Mother-tongue education is globally regarded as essential to laying the foundations of intellectual development of children in the first four years of schooling. English and other languages can then be introduced as subjects. In our racist society the need for mother-tongue education grows ever greater. This is because it enables children to associate education and progress with their own languages and thus develop self-confidence, and pride in their language and culture. Thereafter, the choice of the medium of instruction should be a subject of informed discussion at all levels of education to give young people the best options for their personal and career development.

The selection and training of teachers needs to be overhauled to ensure that only those 'called' to the nurturing of our children are placed in that role. The quality of education is equal to the capacity of its teachers. We need to incentivise teachers who have lost the passion for the profession to retrain themselves. This would create ample space for those called to the profession to contribute to the rebuilding of our society.

Education and training facilities also need to be rebuilt so that they are places which encourage and engender respectful relationships, creativity and collaborative learning. Models of in-service training by institutions such as the LEAP School and African School of Excellence (ASE) show that superior outcomes are achievable through innovations. These institutions pair experienced, highly motivated teachers with new entrants and provide peer support. When lessons are occasions for sharing knowledge, their efficacy is enhanced.

We need to make teaching a career of choice and not of necessity, as it became during the apartheid days. The task of fostering talent in our children should only be entrusted to those whom we respect and trust. Teaching is a sacred duty to prepare generations of citizens for their future roles of building and sustaining their society. Teachers' salaries and benefits need to be radically reformed to attract and keep the best professionals.

Models of successful education transformation

Over the last twenty years, many ordinary citizens in civil society and the private sector have demonstrated that educational excellence is possible even in the poorest areas. Affordable interventions are enabling the poorest young people to rise above their poverty and develop their talents. Their dreams have become achievable.

The LEAP School is one of these interventions. Founded in January 2004 by John Gilmour (who had been the headmaster at Abbotts College in Claremont, Cape Town), the LEAP School is a multi-campus model of affordable sustainable excellence in education. The first LEAP Science and Maths School opened on a shoestring budget in Pinelands, Cape Town. At the end of 2005 the entire first LEAP matric class graduated (although one student had to rewrite two exams).

In 2007 a LEAP teachers' training programme (now called the LEAP Future Leaders Programme) was begun. This was in response to a severe lack of adequately trained teachers in South Africa. The aim remains to enrol 10 per cent of students from each graduating matric class in LEAP to study education at tertiary level. Future leaders are supported to enable them to study for degrees in education at the various tertiary institutions. They then participate in the LEAP Leaders in Education internship.

There are currently some twenty-five young people in the programme. In 2012 two of the first to qualify as teachers were placed in new LEAP schools.

In 2007 a second LEAP school, serving students from Gugulethu and Crossroads, was established, and in 2008 LEAP 3, serving the community of Alexandra, Johannesburg, welcomed its first students. In 2011 LEAP 4 in Diepsloot, Johannesburg, started and in 2012, LEAP 5 in Jane Furse, Limpopo, and LEAP 6 in Ga-Rankuwa, near Pretoria, opened their doors. In 2013, LEAP 2 launched a satellite Grade 9 class serving students living in Delft.

Over the last eleven years the LEAP Schools have seen their matric class grow from fifteen learners in 2005 to 204 learners across three provinces in 2015. For the first time, in 2015, all six LEAP schools had matric classes. LEAP 1 and 2 in Cape Town and LEAP 5 in Jane Furse all achieved a 100 per cent pass rate with LEAP 3, 4 and 6 obtaining 97 per cent, 94 per cent and 78 per cent pass rates respectively. The chart below compares National Senior Certificate (NSC) statistics with the LEAP Schools' matric performance.

These results prove that no matter how poor and marginalised, any child in South Africa can graduate from high school with a qualification that will give them access to tertiary education. Chil-

Comparing 2015 NSC and LEAP matric results

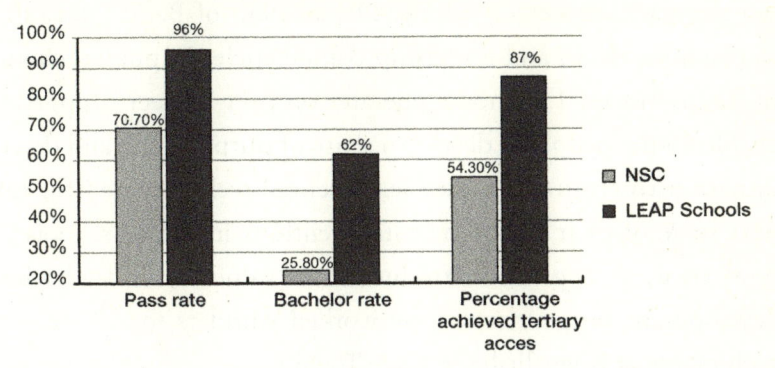

	Pass rate	Bachelor rate	Percentage achieved tertiary access
NSC	70.70%	25.80%	54.30%
LEAP Schools	96%	62%	87%

dren from the poorest communities can and do rise to and exceed all expectations when given a good education by dedicated teachers.

The LEAP School model has inspired an internet-based resource site called Bridge Innovation in Learning and Teaching Network – Bridge, for short. Bridge envisages an education community that is connected, engaged and actively working together to improve the quality of education. To this end it has already become a trusted resource for the management of knowledge, as well as a support centre, especially for those working in difficult isolated places.

An exciting further development of the LEAP School model is the establishment of the Global Teachers Institute (GTI) to transform teacher training approaches. A network of 'extraordinary schools' has, with the support of Bridge, broken the cycle of poor teacher training. The way I see it, the LEAP School graduates are leading the charge to become the innovative teachers of tomorrow. GTI has also partnered with the Department of Higher Education and Training to use the Bridge model to support the government's teacher training initiative, Funza Lushaka.

The Columba Leadership Programme is another success story.

It is a values-based youth leadership programme that has over the last six years partnered with the Department of Basic Education to promote values and leadership competencies in public schools in six provinces. The model operates on peer-to-peer support to enable young people to develop a sense of purpose, grit and determination to ensure that they leave school well prepared for the next stage of their lives. Their interventions in public schools in poor areas, through the introduction of values-based leadership development programmes, have worked wonders for learners in such places as Khayelitsha in Cape Town.

Thanks to Columba, young people who are often left 'to steer by the stars'[4] – in other words, with little guidance but their own innate instincts – are systematically enabled to embrace the values of self-respect and respect for others, and have no fear of the future. Over the last six years Columba Leadership has developed more than 2 400 leaders in ninety schools in seven provinces, mobilising 40 000 beneficiaries. The impact of these values-based young leaders on schools, families and communities has a huge multiplier effect on society.

Yet another example of these interventions is the African School of Excellence, the model for which is rooted in the unique concept of a self-sustaining network of elite independent secondary schools that anyone can afford.[5]

Core to their educational philosophy is that 'Every Child Thinks Perfectly'. In providing a path – through well-researched and exceptionally executed teaching and learning practices – every child is better equipped to lead a productive life.

The teaching approach is 'problem-solving centric', using a rotational classroom methodology:

REIMAGINED EDUCATION AND SKILLS TRAINING

1. Peer-based learning: All ASE lessons feature peer-based learning strategically set in the scholars' Zone of Proximal Development (ZPD). Recent research into developmental psychology has revealed that the best learning occurs just ahead of development, when challenges are too difficult to be comfortable but not so difficult as to cause the scholar to give up. By working in teams on tasks too difficult for any one individual, scholars build on one another's knowledge and simultaneously develop creative problem-solving, analytical reasoning and leadership skills.
2. High-quality instruction: The quality of a school cannot exceed the quality of its teachers. ASE makes sure that each scholar receives quality instruction from a highly trained teacher in every lesson, using a thorough, professionally developed and locally tested lesson plan.
3. Independent practice: Daily independent practice, where the scholar works at the edge of his or her ability, receiving frequent and immediate feedback, has proven to increase learning speed when compared to traditional instruction. Scholars learn to work independently, gaining valuable computer skills and reaching mastery on their own, preparing them for university and beyond.

With an unrelenting focus on academic excellence, ASE has generated promising results. In line with the ASE mission, that graduates succeed at universities both in South Africa and abroad, their scholars write assessments administered by both local and international examination boards.

Interestingly, ASE scholars in Grade 8 wrote Grade 9 exams and their average mathematics score was 38 per cent higher than the

The ASE model

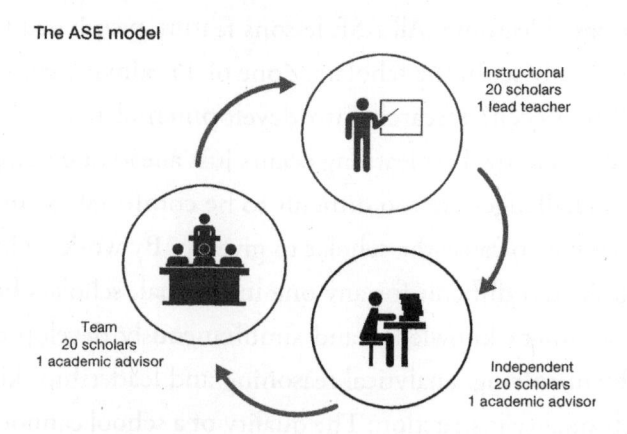

- Instructional: 20 scholars, 1 lead teacher
- Independent: 20 scholars, 1 academic advisor
- Team: 20 scholars, 1 academic advisor

national average. The average home language score was 25 per cent higher than the national average. In maths, more than 90 per cent of ASE Grade 8 scholars performed in the top 10 per cent in the country. Five per cent achieved a score of 80 per cent or more in comparison to the national average of 0.2 per cent.

There is no reason why the ANC government should not have adopted these and other models of success to transform our education and training system. The unpalatable truth is that there may be a view that a poorly educated populace is easier to manipulate and hold hostage than one that is highly educated and skilled. The fewer 'clever blacks' there are, the better for those intent on holding onto power. Could we be witnessing a former liberation movement succumbing to the expediency of keeping the majority in bondage to ignorance and dependency?

How do we reimagine and rebuild a twenty-first-century education and training system?

As I have pointed out, the most effective and efficient way to break the cycle of poverty, inequality and unemployment is by radically transforming our failed education and training system. Ending the betrayal of our children and young people is the most urgent task we face. Without applying our minds to this issue, we will not make our economy more productive, competitive and sustainable.

We have a more youthful population today than ever before. Some 45 per cent of our fifty-four million people are between the ages of fifteen and thirty-nine. This youthful population represents a huge human and intellectual resource that can generate and maintain our socio-economic development. Their talents are sorely needed.

A recent IMF report identifies inclusion of our youthful population in economic development as critical to lifting our economic growth from the estimated zero growth in 2016 to a much higher and sustainable level that would provide benefits to all. The current economic opportunities favour those who have the skills and abilities to be able to creatively engage in generating the necessary goods and services.

I can do no better than draw on the poetic language of David Whyte to capture the opportunity awaiting us:

> Genius is both a gift and a possibility that has not yet occurred ... Genius is the meeting between inheritance and horizon, between what has been told and what can be told, between our practical abilities and our relationship to the gravitational mystery that pulls us on. Our genius is to understand and stand beneath the set of the stars present at our birth, and from that place, to seek the hidden, single star, over the night horizon, we did not know we were following.[6]

South Africa needs to reimagine and rebuild its education system to embrace, encourage and nurture that genius in each child so that it may thrive. This entails enabling everyone 'to seek the hidden, single star, over the night horizon, we did not know we were following'. To paraphrase Whyte, teachers are the people who will make possible each learner's search for the single star they are destined to follow.

Learning is a quest to identify and define your genius and to understand what makes you unique. The learning process involves observation, reflection and practice that generate experience and further learning. Learning understood this way becomes a lifelong quest for how to become better aligned to your 'guiding star' and how to turn the gifts you possess to greater advantage.

Learning exposes you to the range of possibilities and choices that life has to offer. Teachers are 'called' to be inspirational guides for young people to help them find the genius within. Helping teachers to prepare for that role entails leading each teacher on a similar 'journey of discovery'. Our teacher training programmes need to rise to the challenge of preparing teachers to find their own personal strengths so that they can better guide their pupils.

We must invest time and energy in restructuring our education system. The process will need to involve the following: a philosophical and values-based framework for teaching and learning; freely accessible and high-quality education; innovative teaching and learning institutions to promote creative engagement; and integration between education and training involving private sector input.

I'm going to end this segment with insights from two great icons. The first is the poet Maya Angelou, who helps us to distinguish between formal education and learning: 'My mother said I must always be intolerant of ignorance, but understanding of illiteracy. That some people, unable to go to school, were more educated and more intelligent than college professors.'[7] Learning is a lifelong pursuit beyond the formal system of education.

Ignorance in all its forms is intolerable. It is a limitation on the ability to find meaning in your life. It circumscribes the ability of human beings to appreciate their gifts, their potential and their environment in its diversity and complexity. It is well to also remember the other icon, Confucius, who wisely said, 'Ignorance is the night of the mind, but a night without moon and star.'[8] Will we go down in history as a society that failed to root out ignorance by failing to provide an education and training system that lifts the night of the mind and enables all young people to see and follow their lodestars? We need to acknowledge that we have lost our way. We need to reimagine a future school system in which we can believe.

Tertiary education transformation

The cry of young people in our universities has added urgency to the task of transforming our approach to education and training. We need to engage in conversations with students, academics, executive leadership, councils and workers to forge new pathways to a transformed high-performing system of education. The institutional cultures of our universities should be transformed to reflect the values of Ubuntu, non-discrimination and zero tolerance of harassment in any form. Symbols, rituals and ceremonies need to be reviewed to ensure an inclusive celebration of unity in diversity.

The academic process needs radical transformation to ensure

that curriculums, methods of teaching and research reflect the priorities of a society that is rebuilding itself. African history, African languages and culture, as well as a more critical approach to economic theory and business studies, must become part of the core curriculum. Again, it needs to be emphasised, teaching approaches also require radical change. More interactive teaching sessions, smaller groups and peer learning all support creativity and innovation and will enhance the performance of all.

Likewise, we need to transform our reward systems to elevate the teaching of entry-level undergraduates. This would lay a stronger foundation for their academic careers. Teaching needs to be accorded the same status as research if we are to attract the best people who will dedicate more time to tutoring students. The best professors in their fields should be actively involved in teaching to instil the love of their various subjects in young students.

We also need to ensure that the residential facilities of students in higher education become extensions of the lecture theatres, the laboratories and the libraries. The best academic institutions in the US and the UK not only provide affordable high-quality accommodation to all their students, but student residences are mandated as essential to a holistic undergraduate experience. Our highly unequal society and the reality that most of our students are first-generation university entrants, creates a greater imperative to make residences comfortable and safe places for accommodation and learning.

Those calling for online higher education as a preferred path to educating the majority of students are not taking into consideration the importance of education as a critical opportunity to promote the holistic development of young people. Our unequal society cannot be transformed unless we invest in a generation that benefits from this early shaping of their careers and personal development. They need a place that exposes them to social engagement with other young people from different backgrounds. Leaders need to learn and grow together to ensure that they can embed unity in diversity at the core of their beings.

Another priority is to tackle our shockingly high dropout rates, estimated to average 50 per cent of undergraduates in the first year. We should have diagnostic tools that can assess each student entering university, and we should provide them with career counselling as well as academic support to help them pass their subjects. Experience worldwide shows that young people rise to the level of expectations society has of them. We have to understand that young people have gifts that they need to identify and develop in a disciplined manner. We should set high goals and provide the necessary means for them to achieve these standards.

Skills training

Reforming our skills training system is also urgent. Here we could create new hope for the estimated four million young people who are excluded from our economic system. As I have said, abolishing the SETAs would be a start. By all accounts they have failed to produce the skills we need.

The government's unhappiness with the SETAs is multifaceted. They seriously underspend the levy money, while spending disproportionate amounts of their budgets on administrative costs. There are also complaints about the quality of the training that SETAs fund at private sector institutions.[9] Freeing up companies, civil society organisations and the public sector to directly tap into government incentives for employing young people and giving them on-the-job training is both pressing and possible.

We can do no better than learn from the German system that is well regarded internationally. It has been tried and tested and has made that country a resilient high performer even in today's tough global economic climate. The following analysis from *The Atlantic* says it all:

> 'Dual training' captures the idea at the heart of every apprenticeship: Trainees split their days between classroom instruction at a vocational school and on-the-job time at a company. The theory they learn in class is reinforced by the practice at work. They also learn work habits and responsibility and, if all goes well, absorb the culture of the company. Trainees are paid for their time, including in class. The arrangement lasts for two to four years, depending on the sector. And both employer and employee generally hope it will lead to a permanent job – for employers, apprentices are a crucial talent pool.
>
> The first thing you notice about German apprenticeships: The employer and the employee still respect practical work. German firms don't view dual training as something for struggling students or at-risk youth. 'This has nothing to do with corporate social responsibility,' an HR manager at Deutsche Bank told the group I was with, organized by an offshoot of the Goethe Institute. 'I do this because I need talent.' So too at Bosch.
>
> 'Building world-class diesel parts is hard,' the executive in charge of the program explained. 'We're very careful about who we hire. We're looking for quality.' As for trainees, they learn

quickly enough: A mistake on the factory floor is a million-dollar mistake — and they grow up fast, learning not just skills but responsibility. No wonder the apprenticeships are popular: At the John Deere plant in Mannheim, 3,100 young people apply each year for 60 slots, at Deutsche Bank in Frankfurt, it's 22,000 applicants for 425 places.

The second thing you notice: Both employers and employees want more from an apprenticeship than short-term training. Our group heard the same thing in plant after plant: We're teaching more than skills. 'In the future, there will be robots to turn the screws,' one educator told us. 'We don't need workers for that. What we need are people who can solve problems' — skilled, thoughtful, self-reliant employees who understand the company's goals and methods and can improvise when things go wrong or when they see an opportunity to make something work better.[10]

Our government's failure to heed this model over the last twenty-two years has trapped our youth in the hopelessness of poverty, unemployment and inequality. The fear of change and the breaking down of stereotypes about manual work as demeaning requires overcoming the legacy of apartheid's humiliation of black people. Apartheid saw black people as hewers of wood and drawers of water. We need to confront this stigma, acknowledge its pernicious impact on our attitudes to work, and commit ourselves to reframing our relationships to work and the workplace. Healing this wound would unleash creative energy to drive high productivity, co-determination and co-ownership of our economy and ensure its sustainable growth.

Imagine if all local and provincial authorities were to provide apprenticeship opportunities for all unemployed graduates and matriculants to hone their skills in positions such as office assistants, technologists and technicians, school and classroom aides, clinic and hospital general workers, police station administration helpers, public facility maintenance workers, carpenters, plumbers, electricians, road and pavements builders, and library and archive assistants. The list is endless. The pay-off would be igniting hope in young people and enabling them to take ownership of their own development as well as that of their towns, cities and villages.

A reimagined 'second-chance education and training programme' would significantly improve the sense of self-worth and self-respect of young people. The hopelessness that envelops them each time they fail to get a job robs them of dignity and confidence. With the backing of a system that developed their talent and the utilisation of that talent, their lifestyles would be significantly enhanced and we would reduce such social ills as drug and alcohol abuse, unplanned pregnancies and the spread of HIV/AIDS. We would see the benefit both in individuals and in society.

The real opportunity for our society lies in realising that every social problem we have also has its solution. Our sophisticated science and technology base needs to be harnessed and brought into deeper collaborative relationships with the private sector to drive a shift to higher-value manufacturing and service sectors. Our unemployment statistics suggest an opportunity to bring young people into a dynamic workplace by providing them with holistic on-the-job training opportunities. If we can get this right we will be well on our way to a prosperous future.

CHAPTER 9

Reimagining and renewing our cities

Cities and major urban centres are increasingly being recognised as the most important nodes of development of nations in the current century. Africa with its growing young population needs to take deliberate policy actions and invest in reimagining its cities to become attractive socio-economic hubs.

The 'African Economic Outlook 2016' report by the African Development Bank, the United Nations Development Programme and the Organisation for Economic Co-operation and Development points to the enormous opportunities for Africa to transform its under-resourced sprawling cities into vibrant multi-use neighbourhoods.[1] An estimated 800 million of Africa's billion-plus citizens currently live in poverty and squalor on the peripheries of its cities. Unleashing this potentially rich resource of skills, creativity and consumer power would transform our continent into a powerhouse.

South Africa has the greatest opportunity to use its strong institutions to accelerate its development and create more inclusive cities. Citizens spoke with a resounding voice in the 2016 local municipal elections for change in their living conditions and in the appalling quality of public services. Of the eight major metros, only one was won outright by the governing ANC. The main opposition party, the DA, in coalition with other parties, took control in three symbolically important metros: Nelson Mandela Bay – the home of the ANC; Johannesburg – the financial capital; and Tshwane – the nation's capital.

The drop in overall voter support in the 2016 local elections has humbled the ANC for the first time in twenty-three years in power. I can only hope that this will lead to introspection and the rediscovery of its ideals as a liberation party that significantly contributed to the foundations of our democracy. The ANC's support is down from 62 per cent in the 2014 elections to its lowest level since 1994, at 54 per cent.

The era of coalition government politics is likely to strengthen accountability by enhancing competition for voter support among the political parties. Both the DA and the ANC are under greater pressure to demonstrate their capacity to respond effectively to voter expectations that freedom will translate into real socio-economic change for the better in their lives.

It is an opportune time to rethink our cities beyond the apartheid city model that has been perpetuated across the country by all political parties. The apartheid city makes poverty expensive for the majority of people who are poor. It also undermines our national development in multiple ways: individuals, households and the productivity of businesses suffer from the direct and indirect costs of long commutes in our sprawling cities. The challenges of transforming our cities bear within them the opportunities for massive economic growth.

The 'African Economic Outlook 2016' report on African cities identifies urbanisation as an important way of achieving sustainable development. It specifically points to the need for new strategic policies to promote development in three spheres:
- Economic development through higher agricultural productivity, industrialisation, more productive urban services and foreign direct investments;
- Social development by providing cost-effective transport systems, safer housing, social safety nets, social businesses on a larger scale and safer cities; and
- Environmental development by sustainably managing natural resources, notably by providing access to renewable energy, safe water and sanitation, and sustainable waste removal.

We also need to learn from countries that have had to reimagine their urban and housing models to rid their cities of slums and shacks and modernise the city infrastructure to serve all citizens. Ireland has completely eradicated poverty and inequality to turn itself into a modern, vibrant society. The most important policy tool was to utilise the granting of licences to developers on the condition that they built social housing before implementing their own developments. This enabled the local authority to utilise the best expertise to provide quality housing for poor people and accelerate the provision of integrated housing.

This model also operates in other countries with great success. We only have to compare it to our wasteful RDP housing that continues the unsightly and unsustainable urban sprawl that confines poor people to the periphery of our cities to see how we have failed in this area. The RDP housing process is thoroughly corrupt and in the main provides unacceptable inferior housing units. Many of the projects pay little attention to quality physical and social infrastructure, resulting in dysfunctional neighbourhoods.

It is encouraging that Gauteng premier David Makhura admitted in his state of the province address in 2015 that RDP housing was an incubator of poverty. He promised: 'We are doing away with poverty-stricken human settlements in which the day [after taking possession of a house] people have nowhere to go. What's called "RDP houses" is a bad dream. There are no trees, no proper infrastructure and no integration.'[2]

The RDP 'bad dream' is not only a wasted opportunity, but a betrayal of poor people whose dignity continues to be trampled upon by a government that claims success. As Makhura admitted, the concern was with increasing the number of houses built with little regard to the efficient use of land and sustainable economic activity.

According to a 2015 Institute of Race Relations report titled 'South Africa's Housing Conundrum', informal settlements have increased from 300 in 1994 to more than 2200, a more than 650 per cent increase.[3] The cost of RDP houses, despite their persistent poor quality, has increased from R12 500 in 1996 to R160 500. The only beneficiaries of this 'bad dream' are the politically connected tenderpreneurs who are 'top slicing' the grants to build themselves large homes and buy expensive cars before using the small change to provide a shack masquerading as a house.

Despite these damning reports, minister of human settlements Lindiwe Sisulu continued the government's 'good story to tell' in her 2016/17 budget speech: 'We can confirm that since 1994, 4.3 million houses and subsidies have been delivered, providing shelter to over 20 million South Africans, making us number one in the world. These consist of 2.8 million completed houses, 986 000 serviced sites, and 121 000 social housing units. It also includes more than 360 000 households who took the opportunity to acquire ownership of their previously state owned rental properties, 69 000 upgraded community rental units, and 6 000 finance linked subsidies. Government is estimated to have spent over R500 billion for top structures, bulk services, social and economic amenities to achieve this.'[4]

We need to snap out of this bad dream and reimagine our cities and housing development models. We can stop the betrayal and reset our society on a more sustainable development pathway. We have a huge backlog of infrastructure development that is crying out for attention. Most inner-city and township streets, pavements, water and sanitation infrastructure is in an advanced state of disrepair. Imagine how many on-the-job opportunities we could create by just renewing our city infrastructure and laying new infrastructure for reimagined cities? Imagine what a huge boost that would give to our economic development? Remember China's miracle was partly built on infrastructure development. We can also learn from their excesses and be wiser.

For instance, there are ways in which we could reimagine two key cities in our country (Cape Town and Johannesburg) as examples of what is possible.

Cape Town reimagined

Imagine Cape Town in 2025 having completely shed its apartheid geography. Greater Cape Town's current population is nearly four million people. Of those, 69 per cent make up the working population, children account for 25 per cent and there is a small aged group of about 6 per cent. The projected population growth of the Cape metro is 2.1 per cent in 2017, rising to 3.3 per cent in 2020.[5] Imagine a beautiful city abuzz with a diversity of people, a vibrant cultural life and commercial hubs that service locals and tourists. Our city economy would grow by leaps and bounds, and tourism would explode as the world comes to enjoy nature's beauty on the doorstep of a modern integrated city.

This imagined city is a far cry from the current reality. Aerial photographs depict the contrast between the spectacular beauty of the Mother City's iconic landmarks on the one hand and the ugliness of poverty in places like Khayelitsha and Blikkiesdorp on the other. The contrast between the comforts of the coastal suburbs and those at the foot of Table Mountain with those scattered on the sands of the Cape Flats is a painfully humiliating reality for those living on the outskirts of the city. This gap between citizens should encourage us to obliterate from our city the burden of our history.[6]

In her second term, the mayor of Cape Town has an opportunity to lead a process of reimagining our city. The Integrated Development Plan (IDP) is a great way to begin conversations about developing a shared vision of what our city could look like in ten, twenty, thirty years' time. The mayoral committee needs to start by having its own reimagining process so that we can dare to dream together. It is only a re-dreaming process that can lead to the re-emergence of a team approach to implementing the IDP.

The mayor needs to articulate her vision as a starting point for the process. Facilitated group sessions, with residents invited to contribute their visions, would lead to the emergence of a co-owned vision of a reimagined Cape Town. Doing more of the same with the IDP would be to miss an opportunity.

Here are some areas within the city that are ripe for a re-imagined future.

District Six restitution and redevelopment

A reimagined Cape Town would be alive with mixed-use residential areas in all the major corridors. District Six is crying out for development to heal its ugly past. It is unacceptable that all these years into our democracy the forced removal of people from 1966 has still not been redressed. Vacant self-esteem has been a major factor in delays in finalising the restitution of District Six to its original residents or their descendants. The self-sabotaging actions of some of the beneficiaries have contributed to conflicts and confusion as self-interest trumps the common good.

Co-ordinating collaboration between the city, the province and national government has been a challenge. The Cape Town City Council has had its hands full managing the delicate relationships and the unpredictable conflict in the redevelopment process of this prized real estate. In such a fraught situation the temptation by political parties to sabotage the process is ever-present, but must be resisted. The success of a reimagined city is good for everyone and should enable us to transcend party politics. Healing the wounds inflicted by forced removals is in all our interests. A healed District Six would be a powerful visual symbol of the healing of our city, province and nation.

Private developers need to contribute to the rebuilding of District Six by moderating short-term profit motives and by letting a larger vision emerge and be implemented. Succumbing to the temptation of using the easier access to capital by private developers to buy off some of the beneficiaries would undermine the healing process. Consideration of the common good of healing the injustices of forced removals and building our reimagined city together should be paramount. The city needs to look to the Irish experience and insist on private developers only getting licences to develop part of the city contingent on a significant contribution to social housing.

The city needs to consult independent experts, both locally and internationally, to design attractive housing options in a pleasingly planned scheme. Imagine a redesigned, modern District Six as a mixed-use cross-class integrated precinct vibrating with energy. Such a place would have to be developed with the collaboration of beneficiaries bearing in mind the urgency imposed by the rapidly dwindling, ageing population of beneficiaries. Imagine the positive benefit for the Cape Peninsula University of Technology students and staff if they had creative residential spaces as extensions of the academic environment.

The underutilised properties belonging to religious communities, such as the Zonnebloem Education Campus of the Anglican Church, also need to be revamped and extended into multipurpose technical colleges to provide training for inner-city youths. Imagine the vibrancy that would be returned to the city centre, including more inclusive audiences for concerts and other performances that currently are still mostly attended by white people.

Ysterplaat/Century City
Along the N1 the Ysterplaat and Century City precinct could become a booming residential and commercial suburban area with

entry-level housing for young families and single people. Residents of this corridor would be employed or could run their own businesses in designated commercial sectors. Transportation services could be provided using a combination of MyCiTi buses and a revamped Metrorail system. Single-passenger cars would be discouraged because of the frequency of well-integrated public transport.

The challenge would be to align national, provincial and city interests because the land belongs to the South African National Defence Force. The national government would need to put the interests of the nation above those of the ANC, which might be tempted to refuse to collaborate on a programme that would be seen to be bolstering the success of a DA government. The people of South Africa deserve better. All parties should put the citizens of the country first in the healing of the city and its people. Lessons learnt in the process would benefit all other cities.

Muizenberg M5 corridor

The most challenging renewal task would be to restructure the dysfunctional Cape Flats into viable safe neighbourhoods. The Muizenberg M5 corridor needs a major transformation of the gang-infested, unattractive, multi-storey housing complexes into more integrated living spaces. In other words, these flatlands should become residential areas with public parks, sports facilities and shared services such as early childhood development centres and health clinics. Commercial outlets would go a long way to making this area a dignified home for its occupants.

The wounds of forced removals continue to fester in the low-income residential areas along the M5 – Grassy Park, Lavender Hill, Vrygrond, Retreat, etc. – and the social problems here are evident. The run-down, council-owned multi-storey flats with few communal facilities or landscaping could be redeveloped into decent residential areas. The good news is that the same corridor also runs through attractive suburbs such as Plumstead, Marina Da Gama and the Capricorn commercial hub, which could become the pillars of the rebuilding process.

A facilitated process involving participants from the poor areas could open the way for a co-creation of a mixed-use corridor leading to the popular tourist area of Muizenberg. The inclusion of short and medium infrastructure and waste management programmes would offer hope through opportunities for on-the-job training and longer-term maintenance work by the young people in the corridor.

Gugulethu/Manenberg/Klipfontein corridor

The same applies to the Gugulethu/Manenberg/Heideveld/Gatesville and Athlone/Klipfontein Road corridor. This corridor has a rich array of commercial and public service facilities that could benefit from a total reimagining and restructuring. Manenberg's dilapidated multi-storey flats are dysfunctional and have become breeding grounds for gangsterism, drug dealing, and drug and alcohol abuse.

Even the schools remain in the same old pre-fab structures erected by the apartheid government in 1966 as part of the removal and destruction of the District Six community. It is time to put this humiliating legacy behind us and reunite the city. A facilitated reimagining process involving all the role-players, including NGOs that have been working in these townships, could open a window of hope for a co-owned vision of the future.

Nyanga/Crossroads

Nyanga, Crossroads and the vast informal settlements along the N2 pose a major challenge but also a great opportunity to remove an eyesore that would immediately reshape the look and feel of the Mother City. This is a major poverty corridor with very high levels of violent crime. Nyanga is known as the murder capital of the country. Much of the violent crime here involves people known to one another.

Nyanga's rich history of resistance against the anti-urbanisation policies of the apartheid regime should be recalled to mobilise the community to reimagine and rebuild their residential spaces into vibrant and safe quarters. Careful facilitation of genuine community participation, including the voices of angry young people, is essential to craft a shared vision. Healing conversations to enable all voices to be heard would need careful facilitation. It is my belief that win-win scenarios could incentivise the most resistant people to be part of the solution to build an inclusive city.

Bonteheuwel/Bishop Lavis/Langa/Maitland corridor

The other large segment would involve the areas of Bonteheuwel, Bishop Lavis, Langa, Epping, Maitland and Elsie's River. This corridor has a large potential for successful renewal into a mixed-use residential, commercial and industrial development. It has the advantage of major arteries of commerce in nearby highways, rail and MyCiTi bus routes. It also has the potential of bridging the class and ethnic divides to recapture the vibrant culture of the Maitland and Langa of old.

Delft/Blue Downs/Blikkiesdorp

This area presents a major, emotionally charged problem. Promises made to those living in Blikkiesdorp – consisting of 1 600 one-room, eighteen-square-metre structures with appalling sanitation services – have wounded an already humiliated people. Residents of Blikkiesdorp feel that they were dumped there in 2007 to tidy the N2 corridor in preparation for hosting the 2010 FIFA World Cup. The promise that these were temporary shelters while they awaited better housing has yet to be realised. If anything, further numbers of discarded people continue to be dumped there. It is not unreasonable to find alternative, more dignified homes for them in a reimagined and redeveloped city.

Blikkiesdorp needs to be completely abandoned. It is an affront to everything that our human rights–infused constitutional democracy stands for. No child should be condemned to grow up in an environment that violates every one of his or her rights, as Blikkiesdorp does. How can we tolerate another case of the 'discarded people' that Cosmas Desmond documented in Dimbaza in the Eastern Cape during the apartheid era? Like Blikkiesdorp, those dumped in Dimbaza were unwanted people who did not fit into any existing government plan. Can we really discard people in post-apartheid Cape Town and claim it is a well-run city?

Philippi precinct

This quarter offers exciting possibilities for Cape Town to become a food-secure city with vibrant organic agribusinesses that generate sustainable jobs and supply food to the rest of the country and beyond. Careful planning could also turn the Philippi area into a green lung for the city by utilising modern technology that exponentially enhances the productivity of the land, however small.

Converting the recently renovated cement factory into a hub for entrepreneurship needs to be made the core of a reimagined Philippi. Cape Town and its peninsula are already home to technology hubs generating exciting opportunities for creative young people. Developing mixed-use precincts such as Philippi would make the city an affordable place for young families.

The shared vision that emerges from these multiple reimagining processes needs to become a framework for the future development of the city. The process of slum clearance and redevelopment would have to be inclusive and be facilitated by highly trusted experts who will guide the residents, the city, the province and national government departments to collaborate in this social re-engineering programme. We can no longer look the other way as children are born and bred in unsavoury, humiliating places.

The indignities of growing up in places sunk in multi-generational poverty can only be broken by bold commitments from the mayor, the city council and all the residents of Cape Town. We stand to gain much more from a truly inclusive city than from the short-term property deals currently enriching a minority of well-connected people. We have an opportunity for the Mother City to be a model of inclusivity.

Reimagining Johannesburg

Our financial capital has many opportunities to reimagine itself into a modern, inclusive twenty-first-century city, particularly in the inner city and the Alexandra/Sandton areas.

The inner city reimagined

Imagine the inner city of Johannesburg being as vibrant as New York, London and Munich! It is possible. It requires us to go beyond the narrow confines of 'the burden of our history' to embrace a model of integrated mixed-use neighbourhoods where our unity in diversity can be showcased.

Mayor Herman Mashaba's vision is that of an inner city alive with small businesses that flourish and create permanent jobs. He intends to turn the inner city into a safe, vibrant and prosperous space for residents, small businesses and institutions. And to do this he is including all stakeholders in a process that ensures that a reimagined inner city is a shared vision. He says that this is 'vital in our quest to unleash Johannesburg's economic potential and realise a minimum of 5% economic growth ... Our vision must be centred on bringing people and businesses back into our inner city, ultimately benefiting the poorest residents.'[7]

It is refreshing to imagine how local government could use the buildings it owns in the inner city to shape future mixed-use infrastructure in order to redefine what a modern African city could look like. The additional variable of making inner-city development licences contingent on the remodelling of designated buildings into social housing would be the game-changer. The private sector must be given an opportunity to demonstrate its capacity to contribute to 'dealing with the burden of our history' and securing a future where their returns on investment would be beneficial to everyone.

Alexandra township – the burden of history that won't go away

The biggest historic opportunity for Mayor Mashaba is to finally transform Alexandra to be the cosmopolitan twin of its neighbouring sister suburb, Sandton. This will require a complete reimagining of Alex and the rethinking of many failed transformation attempts.

The capture of Alex by criminal and patronage networks would need to be dealt with. The self-sabotaging culture of people who have been humiliated for so long would need to be tackled head on. Well-facilitated healing conversations to enable them to believe in the future are critical to this process. Changing a culture of dependency and mistrust into one of trust and interdependency will be a long and painful journey, but worth the effort to secure a shared future.

There is also an opportunity for the business community in Sandton to become active participants in turning Alex into a vibrant, well-developed suburb with modern mixed-use facilities and residential areas. Dealing with the burden of our history should be a shared process that rebuilds trust. The stories that are yet to be told and heard are the medium of healing the wounds of forced removals and dispossessions that have created a gulf beyond the highway separating the two areas.

Imagine a combination of the rich cultural heritage of Alex and the ultra-modern suburban culture of Sandton coming together into a true South African mix. It would be anything a combination of SoHo and Manhattan in New York City could offer, and beyond what London's West End and the metropole currently provide.

The scars of the City of Gold

The Gauteng landscape is scarred by the complex legacy of apartheid, most visible in the unsound mining practices that resulted in mine dumps. The people of Soweto and other Witwatersrand townships bear the burden of dust and other toxic elements in the air they breathe and the water they drink. It is unclear what the medium- to long-term strategic plan is to address this major environmental and public health challenge by the government at the national, provincial and local level.

The mining industry should be held accountable for its destructive extractive mining practices that have cumulatively benefited a few at the expense of the majority. Emotional settlement discussions need to address how to heal the scars on the land from extractive practices that enriched multiple generations of families and companies. Accountability for healing our landscapes needs to be shared between those who benefited from the huge mineral resources extracted from our land and the public purse. Healing the land is symbolically important for all citizens as part of the national healing project.

The mayor of Johannesburg has a historic opportunity to initiate conversations involving all the major parties: national, provincial and local government leaders together with leaders of the mining industry. Such conversations should enable parties to reimagine what a more sustainable environment could look like. Acknowledgement of the consequences of unsustainable practices, including dusty mine dumps and acid mine drainage, would be at the top of this agenda. It is a burden of our history that we cannot in clear conscience leave for future generations.

A reimagined Johannesburg that cares deeply about the safety, health and prosperity of all its citizens needs to turn to modern technology to find sustainable solutions to the mine-dump problem.[8] There are technological solutions that could generate multiple benefits including attractive economic and financial returns from the residual gold and rare metals in the dumps. There would be training and job opportunities that flow from tackling this age-old problem and these would turn the challenges into attractive prospects. Future generations would be the greatest beneficiaries.

Abandoning the confines of our historical mental and emotional maps is an essential step in reimagining our cityscapes as places of growth and sustenance. The City of Gold as the pioneer of our economic development over the last 130 years has a historic opportunity to lead the way in reimagining our urban landscapes. This is the opportunity South Africa cannot miss.

Conclusion:
Re-dreaming South Africa

South Africa can be likened to a three-legged pot. It stands on one very strong leg – the constitution resulting from our 1994 political settlement. It has a short second leg – the proposed 'socio-economic settlement' which is built on a strong private sector grounded in science and technology. The leg is short because it does not include the talents and creativity of most of the population. They have been left out of the process of building our economy. The shortness of this leg brings instability to the pot. But even more destabilising is the missing third leg – an 'emotional settlement' that can only be attained through reckoning with our painful past and healing our wounds, thereby unleashing the talents of all citizens.

We need to learn the wisdom of Africa in the choice of the three-legged pot as a cooking tool. Structures that rest on three legs are comfortably stable. There is no wobble, no insecurity. South Africa as a well-balanced three-legged pot would be a formidably high-

CONCLUSION: RE-DREAMING SOUTH AFRICA

performing and stable society. It would be fired by the passion of a reimagined country its citizens have co-dreamt and now co-own. A self-sustaining fire would ensure that enough food was cooked well and kept warm for present generations, as well as for those still to be born. It would be a potjie that inspires others as we inspired the world in 1994 with our political settlement under difficult conditions.

Our political settlement delivered a strong leg for our democracy to stand on. The strong leg of our national constitution and its array of mandated institutions, as well as an independent judiciary, have helped us navigate the last two decades. We need to institutionalise a civic education system to ensure that all citizens are competent to assert their rights and assume their responsibilities. Citizens who are confident about their role in a constitutional democracy would have the self-esteem to use their voices knowing they will be heard.

There can be no better way of strengthening the foundations of our democracy than by reaffirming and recommitting to the four imperatives of the preamble of our constitution:

- Heal the divisions of the past and establish a society based on democratic rights, social justice and fundamental human rights;
- Lay the foundations of a democratic open society in which government is based on the will of the people and every citizen is equally protected by law;
- Improve the quality of life of all citizens and free the potential of each person; and
- Build a united and democratic South Africa able to take its place as a sovereign state in the family of nations.

CONCLUSION: RE-DREAMING SOUTH AFRICA

There can be little progress in our transition to democracy unless the 1994 political settlement is complemented by the emotional and socio-economic settlements I have proposed. Healing the wounds of the past that continue to divide us, and establishing a society based on democratic values and human rights, requires intensive work to shift attitudes and social relationships. We need to learn anew how to live together beyond race, gender and class divisions framed by our ugly past.

The experiences of the children of Holocaust victims and victimisers could help inspire us to understand the importance of confronting the past in order to detoxify it. As one of these children put it: 'one revisits the source of pain by speaking about it, analysing its impact on individual's perception of psycho-social life, his/her religious perspective and his/her view of the other'.[1] The question facing us today is: are we willing to revisit the source of the excruciating pain many continue to experience?

Without revisiting the source of pain and anger and speaking about that past it will be difficult to nullify its ability to poison our present and future. It is the inherent venom that is unleashing the self-sabotaging violent protests we witness today that have so disrupted our tertiary education. An emotional settlement is possible only if we are prepared to engage in the difficult healing conversations needed to come to terms with the burden of our history. Victims and victimisers need to acknowledge their woundedness. We need to draw on the rich African philosophical underpinnings of Ubuntu to engage in the acknowledgement of wrongdoing and the forgiveness by those wronged. Only by doing this will we set ourselves on a path to healing our nation's soul.

We need conversations between public and private sector

managers, workers and other stakeholders in the economy to 'detoxify the issues involved so that further exploration and understanding can occur without the psychic barriers that block self-understanding ... The work of memory consists of renewing the past through new experiences, new circumstances, new wonders or horrors of real life.'[2] The work of renewing the past is critically important so that we can hand it over to the next generations as a source of inspiration and not a millstone around their necks. That work is our responsibility to our children's children. We dare not avoid it.

The culture of corruption in the public and private sectors, as well as anti-competitive practices within our corporate sector, is an indication of our failure to co-own our democracy. You cannot steal from yourself. Those corrupt in both the public and private sectors see themselves as outsiders to the system of co-ownership that a constitutional democracy is all about. The ANC government continues to wrestle with its sense of entitlement to state resources 'because we liberated you'. It has yet to make the transition from a liberation movement to a party in a democratic government. It is this sense of entitlement that undermines the emergence of a culture of accountability.

The culture of entitlement to state resources also silences citizens who should be holding those in public office to account. Many black citizens have over the years felt that it would be disloyal to their liberators to publicly criticise this abuse of public resources, starting with the 'arms deal' of the 1990s. The evidence is compelling that the ANC and its key leaders were the main beneficiaries of that deal. There can be no other justification to spend billions on arms without any credible threat to our nation's security.[3] A former MP, Andrew Feinstein, lost a valiant fight to hold those involved in this deal accountable, because the majority of the citizens did not support him.

Some citizens even think it's only human to repay yourself for all those years of sacrifice during the struggle. Who can forget the infamous statement in 2004 by Smuts Ngonyama, then a key figure in the Mbeki presidency, who said, 'I did not join the struggle to be poor'?[4] There is nothing wrong with this at face value, except that Ngonyama was facilitating a Telkom BEE deal and stood to benefit personally.

Many white people feel that it is not appropriate for them to raise their voices to hold public leaders accountable. The burden of their complicity and the benefits they derived from apartheid weighs heavily on them, undermining their citizenship roles. They need healing to free themselves from guilt, shame and fear of marginalisation to make the final journey of taking ownership of the democracy. 'We the People' can only ring true when we all unburden ourselves to rise to our responsibilities.

Embracing an emotional settlement process would help us 'work through' the pain, anger and sense of loss on the part of survivors of apartheid. We would free ourselves from the burden of history. Similarly, the perpetrators and beneficiaries of apartheid need to be freed from the guilt, shame and denialism that currently paralyse so many of them. White corporate leaders need to heal themselves and assume responsibility as corporate citizens. This would help to stem the tide of illicit financial flows into 'safe havens' abroad as insurance against the uncertainties of our future. These safety nets are undermining our economic sustainability.

We need the private sector to engender a more inclusive economy. It is impossible to build a strong sustainable economy when only 20 per cent of the population is involved. Working together to build an economy that includes the majority – black people, women and the youth – makes sense for anyone committed to contributing towards a more prosperous future.

Inclusion would build greater trust between black and white citizens, between producers and consumers of goods and services, and this would enhance productivity and create higher growth rates. Compliance-motivated BEE deals have not delivered, and will not deliver, the needed momentum to fundamentally restructure our socio-economic system into an inclusive one.

What is needed is a 'reading of the scars'[5] of exploitative economic practices, including the iniquitous migrant labour system. This system has undermined African family life for the past 150 years. We cannot afford to keep averting our eyes from those deep scars. We need to commit ourselves to creating more dignified working and living environments. Such places would nurture more trusting, mutually respectful corporate cultures free of harassment in any form: racial, sexual and other forms of discrimination. Respectful corporate cultures would enable businesses to promote co-created and co-owned sustainable approaches.

There is a growing chorus of young white voices wanting change, including this Grade 10 pupil in KwaZulu-Natal who wrote to her headmaster expressing her vision of the future: 'Our aim is to educate people on the issue of privilege in South Africa, to open a safe space for people to discuss their doubts, questions and opinions regarding this issue and ultimately, to remind the youth that they are going to be responsible for South Africa one day, warts and all. It is up to us to transform this nation into what we know it can be.'

CONCLUSION: RE-DREAMING SOUTH AFRICA

Healing is essential to enabling empathy to flow within our unequal society and to help us acknowledge that inequality is expensive for both rich and poor. It is out of such recognition that we can commit ourselves to a fundamental restructuring of our social system to create a stronger, longer third leg to rebalance the national potjie: a socio-economic settlement. Such a settlement would enable us to eradicate poverty and stimulate our economic growth rates into the high-performance category.

Our society has the resources we need to invest in all citizens' access to the sort of quality public services that would ensure the development of strong human and intellectual capital. What is needed is to reorder our priorities to ensure that we stop the leakage of public funds through corruption, maladministration and incompetence. Eliminating the estimated 30 to 40 per cent of the R600 billion procurement budget that is lost due to corruption, nepotism and maladministration would make available between R180 and R240 billion for the investments needed to unleash the talents and energies of all citizens. Eliminating illicit financial outflows would also make available a further estimated R300 billion of taxable income.

South Africa is being given another opportunity to reckon with the past. We have the pressure from young people who want to see a reimagined society recommitting itself to mobilising all citizens to rebuild the prosperous democracy promised in 1994. We need to rise to the occasion and reignite hope. The beauty of imagination is that it enables us to get ahead of ourselves and to start living the reimagined future we yearn to build together.

Reimagining my country enables me to live in the future I yearn for. I no longer feel that I am holding a solitary grain of sand

CONCLUSION: RE-DREAMING SOUTH AFRICA

in my hand. Many more hands have linked together to ride wave after wave of hope. The golden sea sand tumbles in the waves, no longer as single grains. The wealth of the possibilities of our imagined future is like the myriad golden grains of sand on never-ending expansive seashores. The dream is alive.

Notes

PROLOGUE
1. Human Sciences Research Council, 'Policy Framework on Social Security for Youth in South Africa', Final Report, March 2012.
2. 'Report of the Working Group on Values in Education', 9 May 2000, available at http://www.gov.za/sites/www.gov.za/files/Report%20of%20the%20 Working%20Group%20on%20Values%20in%20Education_0.pdf (last accessed 17 January 2017).
3. Department of Education, 'Values, Education and Democracy', 2000, p. 4, available at http://www.education.gov.za/Portals/0/DoE%20Branches/ Social%20and%20School%20Enrichment/Race_and_Values/values%202000. pdf?ver=2008-06-30-154303-337 (last accessed 17 January 2017).
4. Cheikh Anta Diop, *Civilization or Barbarism: An Authentic Anthropology* (New York: Lawrence Hill, 1974), p. 375.
5. Ibid., p. 212.

CHAPTER 1: CHASING A DREAM WITHIN THE DREAM
1. Stephen B. Biko, *Frank Talk: I Write What I Like* (Johannesburg: Picador Africa, 2004), pp. 101–102.
2. John Henrik Clarke, available at http://www.azquotes.com/quote/882885 (last accessed 18 January 2017).
3. Niccolò Machiavelli, available at https://bieberlabs.com/2007/06/01/the-myths-

of-innovation-and-the-full-machiavelli-quote-on-change (last accessed 18 January 2017).
4. Verashni Pillay, 'Pansy Tlakula's IEC lease was irregular, says Madonsela', *Mail & Guardian*, 26 August 2013.

CHAPTER 2: HISTORY MATTERS
1. Diop, *Civilization or Barbarism*, p. 2.
2. Alta Engelbrecht, 'The impact of role reversal in representational practices in history textbooks after apartheid', *South African Journal of Education*, 28(4): 519–541.
3. Elize S. van Eeden, 'South Africa's revised history curriculum on globalism and national narratives in grade 12 textbooks', *Historia*, 55(1): May 2010.
4. See Antjie Krog, *Begging to Be Black* (Cape Town: Random House Struik, 2009).
5. Eric Wolf, *Europe and the People Without History* (Jackson: University of California Press, 1982).
6. Diop, *Civilization or Barbarism*, p. 212.
7. Cheikh Anta Diop, *The African Origin of Civilization: Myth or Reality* (New York: Lawrence Hill, 1974).
8. Cecil John Rhodes, 'Confession of Faith' (1877), in John E. Flint, *Cecil Rhodes* (Boston: Little Brown, 1974), pp. 248–52.
9. A. Moore, '10 black scholars who debunked Eurocentric propaganda', *Atlanta Black Star*, 6 October 2013, available at http://atlantablackstar.com/2013/10/06/10-black-scholars-debunked-eurocentric-propaganda/ (last accessed 18 January 2017).
10. Joy DeGruy, *Post Traumatic Slave Syndrome: America's Legacy of Enduring Injury and Healing* (Alberta: Joy DeGruy Publications, 2005).

CHAPTER 3: WHAT'S IN A NAME?
1. Statement to the police by Puis Nomgcana, 24 January 2014.

CHAPTER 4: THE BIGGEST BETRAYAL
1. Victoria John, 'Forgotten schools of the Eastern Cape left to rot', *Mail & Guardian*, 8 March 2013.
2. O. Shisana, K.F. Peltzer, N.P. Zungu-Dirwayi, J.S. Louw, 'The health of our educators: A focus on HIV/AIDS in South African public schools, 2004/5 survey' (Cape Town: HSRC Press, 2005).
3. Es'kia Mphahlele, *Es'kia* (Cape Town: Kwela, 2002), p. 19.
4. Sipho Masondo, 'Angie Motshekga reads riot act', *City Press*, 24 January 2016.
5. Statistics courtesy of UCT Faculty of Engineering and the Built Environment, November 2016.

NOTES

CHAPTER 5: TIME TO DREAM OURSELVES INTO THE NEW SOUTH AFRICA WE IMAGINED IN 1994

1. Jeff Wicks, '"It's just the facts" – Penny Sparrow breaks her silence', *News24*, 4 January 2016, available at http://www.news24.com/SouthAfrica/News/its-just-the-facts-penny-sparrow-breaks-her-silence-20160104 (last accessed 19 January 2017).
2. Dan Bar-On, *Tell Your Story* (New York: Central European University Press, 2006), p. 217.
3. H. Biko, *The Great African Society: A Plan for a Nation Gone Astray* (Cape Town: Jonathan Ball, 2013), p. 273.
4. Bar-On, *Tell Your Story*, p. 222.
5. Mary-Anne Gontsana, 'Over R1 billion in fund – yet apartheid victims still await compensation', *GroundUp*, 5 November 2013, available at http://www.groundup.org.za/article/over-r1-billion-fund-yet-apartheid-victims-still-await-compensation/ (last accessed 19 January 2017).
6. 'Dan Bar-On', Wikipedia, available at https://en.wikipedia.org/wiki/Dan_Bar-On (last accessed 19 January 2017).
7. Bar-On, *Tell Your Story*, p. 202.
8. Quoted in DeGruy, *Post Traumatic Slave Syndrome*.
9. 'Social pain: A conversation with Naomi Eisenberger', *Edge*, 10 September 2014, available at https://www.edge.org/conversation/naomi_eisenberger-social-pain (last accessed 19 January 2017).
10. Ibid.
11. 'The Wyllie Lynch letter: The making of a slave!', 25 December 1712, available at http://www.itsabouttimebpp.com/bpp_books/pdf/the_willie_lynch_letter_the_making_of_a_slave!.pdf (last accessed 19 January 2017).
12. Frances Cronin, 'Nazi legacy: The troubled descendants', *BBC News*, 23 May 2012, available at http://www.bbc.com/news/magazine-18120890 (last accessed 19 January 2017).

CHAPTER 6: UBUNTU AS A HEALING FRAMEWORK

1. M.O. Eze, *Intellectual History in Contemporary South Africa* (London: Palgrave Macmillan, 2010), pp. 190–191.
2. Nora Bateson, *Small Arcs of Larger Circles* (Axminster: Triarchy, 2016), p. 25.
3. D. Whyte, *Consolations* (Langley WA: Many Rivers Press, 2015).
4. DeGruy, *Post Traumatic Slave Syndrome*.
5. Hugh Macmillan, *The Lusaka Years: The ANC in Exile in Zambia, 1963 to 1994* (Johannesburg: Jacana, 2013).
6. Bar-On, *Tell Your Story*, p. 218.
7. Claude M. Steele and Joshua Aronson, 'Stereotype threat and intellectual testing of African Americans', *Journal of Personality and Social Psychology*, 69(5), 1995, pp. 797–811.

NOTES

8. Gareth van Onselen, 'The DA opens its door to racial quotas', *Business Day*, 12 October 2016.
9. K. Ratele, 'Masculinity and male mortality in South Africa', *African Safety Promotion: A Journal of Injury and Violence Prevention*, 6(2), 2008, pp. 19–41.
10. Gender Links, 'Measuring gender based violence', *Barometer*, 1 February 2011, available at http://genderlinks.org.za/barometer-newsletter/measuring-gender-based-violence-2011-02-01/ (last accessed 25 January 2017).
11. 'Study reveals extent of gender violence', *Brand South Africa*, 5 December 2012.

CHAPTER 7: REBUILDING OUR SOCIETY

1. Thomas Piketty, 13th Nelson Mandela Annual Lecture, 3 October 2015, transcript available at https://www.nelsonmandela.org/news/entry/transcript-of-nelson-mandela-annual-lecture-2015 (last accessed 25 January 2017).
2. R. Wilkinson and K. Pickett, *The Spirit Level: Why Equality is Better for Everyone* (London: Penguin Books, 2010).
3. Piketty, 13th Nelson Mandela Annual Lecture.
4. 'Inclusive economy will lift SA, say IMF', *Business Day*, 19 July 2016.
5. C.M. Purfield, et al., 'South Africa economic update : Promoting faster growth and poverty alleviation through competition', *South Africa Economic Update*, 8 (Washington, DC: World Bank Group, 2016), available at http://documents.worldbank.org/curated/en/917591468185330593/South-Africa-economic-update-promoting-faster-growth-and-poverty-alleviation-through-competition (last accessed 25 January 2017).
6. Katrin Elborgh-Woytek, et al., 'Women, work, and the economy: Macroeconomic gains from gender equity', IMF, September 2013, available at https://www.imf.org/external/pubs/cat/longres.aspx?sk=40915 (last accessed 25 January 2017).
7. McKinsey Global Institute report, September 2015, available at http://www.mckinsey.com/global-themes/employment-and-growth/how-advancing-womens-equality-can-add-12-trillion-to-global-growth (last accessed 25 January 2017).
8. Muhammad Patel, 'Illicit outflow of capital from South Africa eliminated by statutory duties placed on directors', Southern African Legal Information Institute, September 2015, available at http://www.saflii.org/za/journals/DEREBUS/2015/163.html (last accessed 25 January 2017).

CHAPTER 8: REIMAGINED EDUCATION AND SKILLS TRAINING

1. Claudio E. Montenegro and Harry A. Patrinos, "Returns to schooling around the world', Background paper for the World Development Report 2013, available at http://siteresources.worldbank.org/EXTNWDR2013/Resources/8258024-1320950747192/8260293-1320956712276/8261091-1348683883703/WDR2013_bp_Returns_to_Schooling_around_the_World.pdf (last accessed 25 January 2017).

2. Harry A. Patrinos, '50 years of "Returns to Education" studies', Education for Global Development blog, 19 March 2015, available at http://blogs.worldbank.org/education/50-years-returns-education-studies (last accessed 25 January 2017).
3. Mphahele, *Es'kia*, p. 79.
4. A metaphor borrowed from my book *Steering by the Stars: Being Young in South Africa* (Cape Town: Tafelberg, 2002), a narrative of poor, young black people in South Africa's New Crossroads in Cape Town.
5. The ASE profile and model were provided by the founders and team of the ASE and used here with their permission.
6. Whyte, *Consolations*.
7. Maya Angelou, available at https://www.brainyquote.com/quotes/quotes/m/mayaangelo148652.html (last accessed 26 January 2017).
8. Confucius, available at http://www.quotationspage.com/quote/28879.html (last accessed 26 January 2017).
9. Dewald van Rensburg, 'Blade Nzimande set to scrap the Setas', *City Press*, 15 November 2015.
10. Tamar Jacoby, 'Why Germany is so much better at training its workers', *The Atlantic*, 16 October 2014.

CHAPTER 9: REIMAGINING AND RENEWING OUR CITIES

1. AfDB, UNDP and OECD, 'African Economic Outlook 2016: Sustainable cities and structural transformation', 15th edition, available at https://www.afdb.org/fileadmin/uploads/afdb/Documents/Publications/AEO_2016_Report_Full_English.pdf (last accessed 26 January 2017).
2. Olebogeng Molatlhwa, 'RDP housing breeds poverty, says Makhura', *TimesLive*, 8 April 2015.
3. Institute of Race Relations, 'South Africa's Housing Conundrum', @Liberty policy bulletin, 20(4), 6 October 2015.
4. 'Minister Lindiwe Sisulu: Human Settlements Dept Budget Vote 2016/17', Remarks by the Minister of Human Settlements on the occasion of the Budget Vote of the Ministry of Human Settlements, Imbizo Media Centre, Parliament, 3 May 2016.
5. 'Cape Town population 2016', World Population Review, available at http://worldpopulationreview.com/world-cities/cape-town-population/ (last accessed 26 January 2017).
6. 'Urban legacy of apartheid captured in stunning aerial shots', news.com.au, 24 June 2016, available at http://www.news.com.au/news/urban-legacy-of-apartheid-captured-in-stunning-aerial-shots/news-story/ced7ccd48016d4085394 5c68b49e895a (last accessed 26 January 2017).
7. 'Mayor Mashaba moves to re-ignite inner city spark', Joburg.org.za, 15 September 2016, available at http://www.joburg.org.za/index.

php?option=com_content&id=10831&Itemid=266 (last accessed 26 January 2017).
8. See http://www.theblueeconomy.org/ for more information.

CONCLUSION: RE-DREAMING SOUTH AFRICA
1. Allan and Naomi Berger, *Second Generation Voices: Reflections of Holocaust Survivors and Perpetrators* (Syracuse: Syracuse University Press, 2001), p. 6.
2. Ibid., p. 7.
3. Andrew Feinstein, *After the Party: A Personal and Political Journey Inside the ANC* (Johannesburg: Jonathan Ball, 2007).
4. Smuts Ngonyama, available at https://inside-politics.org/2012/04/23/the-ancs-all-time-top-10-most-disturbing-quotes/ (last accessed 26 January 2017).
5. Berger, *Second Generation Voices*, p. 6.

Bibliography

Bar-on, Dan. *Legacy of Silence: Encounters with Children of the Third Reich*. Boston: Harvard University Press, 1991
——— *Tell Your Story*. New York: Central European University Press, 2006
Bateson, Nora. *Small Arcs of Larger Circles*. Axminster: Triarchy, 2016
Berger, Allan and Naomi. *Second Generation Voices: Reflections of Holocaust Survivors and Perpetrators*. Syracuse: Syracuse University Press, 2001
Biko, H. *The Great African Society: A Plan for a Nation Gone Astray*. Cape Town: Jonathan Ball, 2013
Biko, S.B. *Frank Talk: I Write What I Like*. Johannesburg: Picador Africa, 2004
DeGruy, Joy. *Post-Traumatic Slave Syndrome: America's Legacy of Enduring Injury and Healing*. Alberta: Joy DeGruy Publishers, 2005
Diop, Cheikh Anta. *Civilization or Barbarism: An Authentic Anthropology*. New York: Lawrence Hill & Company, 1974
——— *The African Origin of Civilization: Myth or Reality*. New York: Lawrence Hill & Company, 1974

BIBLIOGRAPHY

Eze, M.O. *Intellectual History in Contemporary South Africa.* London: Palgrave Macmillan, 2010
Feinstein, Andrew. *After the Party: A Personal and Political Journey Inside the ANC.* Johannesburg: Jonathan Ball, 2007
Flint, John E. *Cecil Rhodes.* Boston: Little Brown, 1974
Krog, Antjie. *Begging to Be Black.* Cape Town: Random House Struik, 2009
Macmillan, Hugh. *The Lusaka Years: The ANC in Exile in Zambia, 1963-1994.* Johannesburg: Jacana, 2013
Mphahlele, Es'kia. *Es'kia.* Cape Town: Kwela, 2002
Ramphele, Mamphela. *A Passion for Freedom.* Cape Town: Tafelberg, 2013
—— *Steering by the Stars: Being Young in South Africa.* Cape Town: Tafelberg, 2002
Whyte, David. *Consolations.* Langley WA: Many Rivers Press, 2015
Wilkinson, R., and Pickett, K. *The Spirit Level: Why Equality is Better for Everyone.* London: Penguin Books, 2010
Wolf, Eric. *Europe and the People Without History.* Jackson: University of California Press, 1982

Do you have any comments, suggestions or feedback
about this book or any other Penguin titles?
Contact us at **talkback@penguinrandomhouse.co.za**

Visit **www.penguinrandomhouse.co.za** and subscribe
to our newsletter for monthly updates and news